THE DANCE RECITAL

A practical guide for teachers

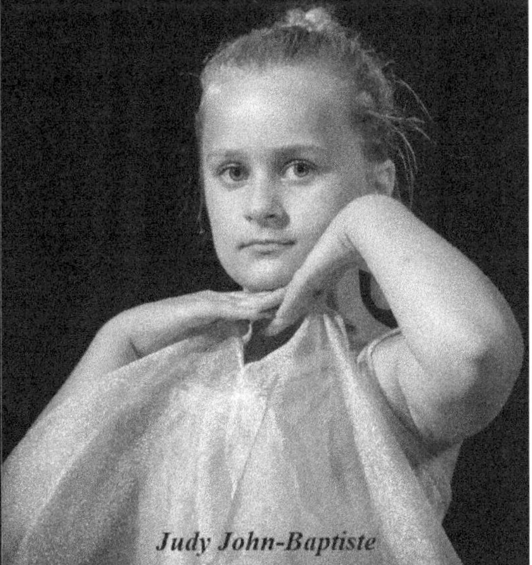

THE DANCE RECITAL

The Dance Recital is an invaluable guide book for dance teachers who are tackling their first dance performance. With the volume of things to remember this book helps to ensure that nothing is left to chance. It will ensure that your dance recital runs effortlessly and earn you the trust and respect of all of your dance pupils.

Judy John-Baptiste

ISBN 978-0-244-62526-9

9 780244 625269

1

THE DANCE RECITAL
A practical guide for teachers

Judy John-Baptiste

For my mum, and my daughter

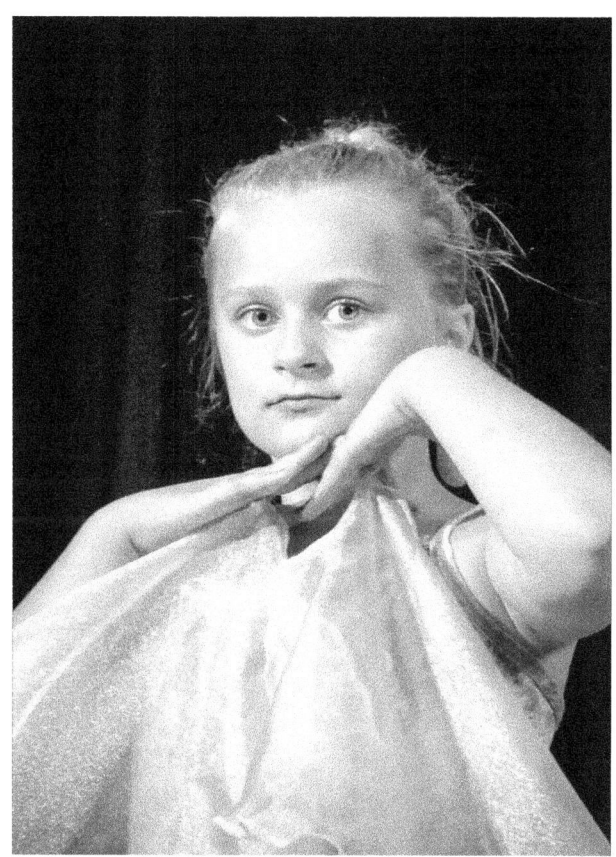

Carmel Jane Photography ©2017

THE DANCE RECITAL: A PRACTICAL GUIDE FOR TEACHERS

Contents

The dance recital: Quite a tall order!

Suddenly the buzz of chatter in the auditorium falls silent. The audience sits silently in the sudden deep darkness of the theatre. The sense of anticipation is almost palpable. The lights slowly flood the stage where nervous dancers are poised waiting for the music to begin. The annual dance recital has just begun. A year of hard work is about to reveal itself on stage.

The dance recital is a live event, and like all live performances once it has commenced there is no going back. But the annual dance school recital is unlike other dance performances. The recital is cast by a group of inexperienced dance pupils undertaking to emulate the dance professional. These daring dancers start to perform from 3 years old. Sometimes they have nothing but a term or two of preschool dance classes under their belt for preparation. Their dance school attendance may eventually stretch over several years, but currently they are dance conscripts. They are beginners, novices, and rookies, all doing their best on stage.

By contrast the professional dancer can boast many years professional study and live performance experience. Slowly, the dancer's body and mind has been crafted for the stage. The professional dancer has been primed for many of the eventualities on stage. But for the dance recital pupil performing their first dance recital, this is unknown territory. So many things to remember, so many things can go wrong. For the dance recital pupil, the dance recital is akin to a daunting precipice; each step is filled with nervous anticipation.

As dance professionals we endeavour to help pupils navigate through the dance concert. A well-thought-out dance performance can help to minimise many of the perils for pupils in performance. A properly structured recital can provide a stable brace for the clutch of pupils who find themselves centre stage with little or no experience. They, understandably are relying on us, the professionals for support, guidance and experience to steer them through the whole process.

Dance recital pupils need assurances that those at the helm are competent leaders.

This book is a practical guide for dance teachers, studio owners and parents who partake in the annual dance recital. It can be used as a reference to plan and execute the dance recital from start to finish. It starts at the beginning with the recital theme, and then explores many of the components that contribute towards a successful dance performance. It examines what to teach, how to teach, and how best to prepare children for dancing on stage. It looks at the practices of back stage management, and gives strategies to maintain order. This book gives ideas on how to generate income from the dance recital and looks at the legal requirements for children in performance.

The Dance Recital is an invaluable guide book for dance teachers who are tackling their first dance performance. With the volume of things to remember, this book helps to ensure that nothing is left to chance. It will ensure that your dance recital runs effortlessly and earns you the trust and respect of all of your dance pupils.

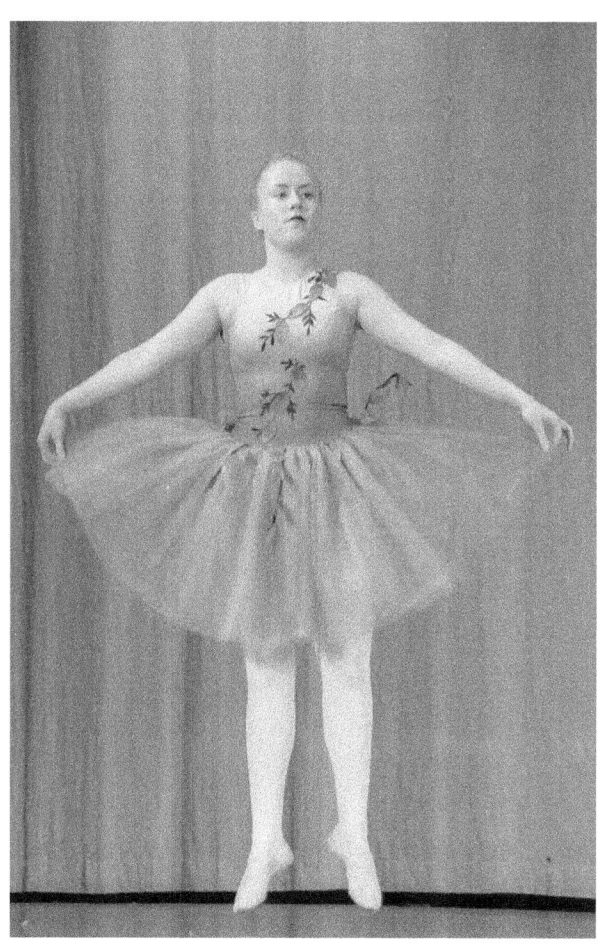

Carmel Jane Photography ©2017

What is a dance recital?

A dance recital is a public display of the artistic expression of a dance school at full tilt. It is the pivotal culmination of a year's dance tuition and training for public observation. It reveals to the public a school's aspirations, growth and student talent and ability. It tells all who are interested what a school represents and stands for.

For all who participate, the recital can be a time to take stock of what has been learned, and assess technical and/or artistic progression in comparison to previous years. The outcome of these considerations may determine whether a student continues training with the same dance school or moves onto pastures new. The student may wonder whether the end of year recital was a true reflection of the physical challenges of training throughout the year. If the performance went well and was well received, the student may feel justified in continuing onto the next year. But if a student experienced frustration in terms of his/ her artistic development, in conjunction with an unfulfilling show, his/her departure may be imminent.

For the teachers, the end of year recital is a very important feature of the dance school's annual calendar. It is the medium through which they are able to demonstrate their choreographic prowess, and to showcase their expertise as teachers through their students on stage. The recital grants them the opportunity to account for their position in a school. It is at the dance recital that they are subject to critical assessments from all sides. The studio owner considers his/her investment and judges whether or not the teacher was a worthy investment for the school. The studio owner, is mindful of how the teacher and her work represents the dance school. Does the work produced by the teacher cohere with the artistic principles of the school? Did the work manage to blend harmoniously with the other contributors? These teachers are significant because they all converge to form the school's identity. The studio owner needs to assess whether the teacher co-operated fully with the themes of the recital or whether he/she was too individualistic and motivated by personal expression and ego.

Woe betide the teacher whose recital contribution is deemed a little too maverick, or has misrepresented the brief. If the work is not well received, a teacher's return to work in the autumn may be in jeopardy. The studio owner is only too aware of his/her competitors. He/she will want assurances that their production is at par with or better than others in the locality. They would like their production to be a beacon for others to emulate. Their competitors are most likely to be their fiercest critics and so they watch over their teaching staff with a supportive but judicious eye.

During the dance recital families and friends are excited to see the fruits of their children's labour. Many schools (although not all) do not permit class viewings throughout the year, so parents are bursting with curiosity to see the product of a year's work. For sure parents are always keen to seen their child perform. But amid all this excitement the parents have some calls to make too. The parents will assess the performance abilities of their children and consider if the artistic capabilities of their children are being fully exploited. Are the teachers sufficiently skilled to maximise their child's abilities and is that apparent on stage? They need to see that their child is ostensibly becoming a talented performer.

Dance recitals will be preserved for years to come via the mobile phone, camcorder or a professionally recorded video for all the family to enjoy. The student will want to experience a sense of pride when these shows are replayed at home. But most significantly, the audience reaction and the overall feedback after the show is a vital marker for the young dancer. A favourable response from an audience is a just prize for the accomplishments achieved through training and dedication over twelve months. Audience approval is an elixir for months of perseverance, hard work and arduous rehearsals.

A lot is riding on the annual recital. With the hopes and fears of all participants, the recital is infused with longings to entertain and impress an audience, who are also hoping for a wonderful, spectacle that meets with expectation or more.

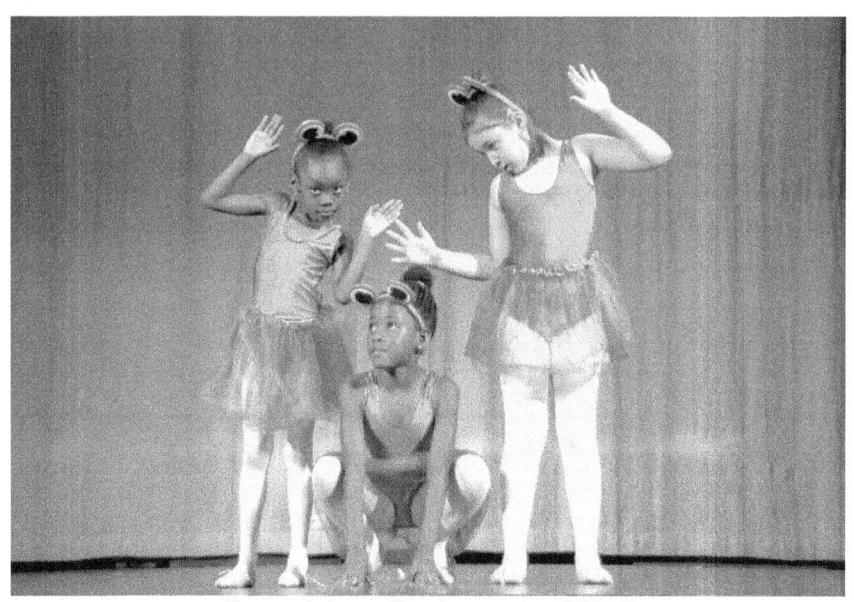

Carmel Jane Photography ©2017

Why choose a recital theme?

Choosing a theme is not essential. The audience members who attend will largely be family members or have some connection to the performers. They will want to see an entertaining production showcasing the developing talents of all who perform. They are barely interested in whether a theme is present or not. But the use of a theme can help to amalgamate a plethora of choreographic works for dancers of varying ages and abilities. When all parts are subsumed under one unifying theme, audience members are more likely to become engaged. They are less likely to look to family members performing on stage as the singular source of their entertainment. They are likely to become engrossed in the narrative theme that permeates the whole show, and more receptive to the presentations of the other dancers.

Deciding upon a theme can at times be a frustrating process. Sometimes there are a flurry of ideas that arrive simultaneously awaiting realisation. These ideas need to be assembled in the form of a choreographic journal for future use. There is no guarantee that the good ideas thought of today will be remembered tomorrow. But still, these burgeoning ideas could be invaluable and may need to be retrieved to supplement other dance works in the future.

A theme needs to inspire the development of several creative permutations. Each participating teacher is unique and will need the freedom to interpret a thematic idea in a manner that is characteristic of his/her style and personality. But at the same time a theme should not be so broad that the theme is virtually imperceptible. It needs to act as an arterial vein connecting all parts.

A theme may also may need to sustain different dance styles. It is very common for dance studios to offer a wide range of dance classes, and all will need to come together on stage. Decisions will need to be made as to whether the interpretations of the theme will be literal, abstract or narrative. Will these issues be left to the judgement of the individual teachers or will those decisions be agreed on in staff meetings? In all events the theme serves to create a seamless connection between all contributing parts, taking care to avoid a disjointed, incoherent production.

Despite the challenges of establishing a theme, there are several benefits. In a large school where there are lots of contributing teachers and dancers, a theme helps to create a cohesive production. Once a theme is agreed, teachers can work within its confines in their own individual artistic way. This can be rewarding for a dance teacher who recognises that he/she is part of a team, but is still afforded the liberty of creative independence. A theme can help to bond pupils in terms of ability, age and experience. From the toddler in pre-ballet to the pre- vocational student, all can participate producing creative material reflective of their dance knowledge. This helps to represent the diversity inherent in some schools while at the same time unifying all its unique individual parts.

A theme is carried through all aspects of the production. The choice of music, lighting, costume and props are all selected with the theme in mind. For these elements to be joined, a schematic representation of needs should be formed by dance teachers with technicians, and those who are responsible for the recital wardrobe.

Considerations for a theme

When contemplating a theme, there are various issues to take into account. The age range of dancers may play a significant role in deciding upon a theme. A large school may have varying ages and abilities, which will have some influence on the final selection. Adolescent students will need to work with ideas that are reflective of their age. Material for this age group needs to be mildly mature but not offensive. In contrast, pre ballet pupils will need material that is playful, endearing and light hearted. With such varying requirements the final theme may involve taking its audience on a journey from the light hearted to the obscure. Whimsical representations of a toy doll for pre ballet may turn dark and become a crazed, diabolical doll for teenage dancers. A fantasy garden full of fairies and pixies created

for pre-ballet pupils might develop into a spooky night garden for mid-teens or an innocent romantic setting for older teenagers.
In all events the theme should be suitable for family viewing and be flexible enough to reflect the different age groups in a dance school.

A theme should provide dancers with the opportunity to showcase their talents and technical accomplishments. After months of practising a pirouette, dancers will want to display this new skill for all to see. Performing new feats can be intimidating but can leave dancers feeling euphoric if carried out successfully. Parents and families are exhilarated when they can clearly observe a marked improvement due to continual dance training over the expanse of a year. Obvious progress gives parents confidence that the school is competent, has a good teaching faculty and signifies that pupils are consistently doing well. Discernible performer improvement can allay dancer aspirations to studio hop. It is not uncommon for students to hit a technical hiatus where improvement begins to stand still and dance students may begin to feel a compelling sense of frustration. Classes begin to feel tiresome and the idea of a new teacher, new surroundings and new challenges may seem the solution to break the stagnation. An exciting and well received recital can expunge all thoughts of departure. A good recital can consolidate a pupil's allegiance to a school, becoming its public advocate. As such it is important to provide a good recital that improves annually. It is imperative that the dance recital provides an opportunity for pupils to display individual talents wherever possible, and the chance to show parents and family members the development of technical and artistic growth.

The recital as a whole should improve annually. Looking critically at the recordings of previous recitals will not only give a good indicator of the ways in which a recital can improve as a production but also how it can showcase its dancers to the fullest. This resource should be made available to teachers and pupils alike. Teachers should embrace the choreographic challenges lurking within the realms of a recital theme with a will to improve each year. It is crucial that teachers are fully on board with a recital theme and are inspired by the production. A teacher who is unimpressed with a theme idea will doubtlessly produce dull, lacklustre choreography. A theme should

16

enthuse teachers sufficiently animating them to produce fulfilling, rewarding work for the stage. To this end it makes good sense that teachers should have some input in establishing a recital theme idea. Doing this awards teachers greater ownership of the recital and elevates their sense of self-worth in the school.

The dance recital should award its dancers the opportunity to demonstrate their technical development. Complex footwork, impressive leaps and partner work are duly welcome and may feature as the highlight of the show. Athleticism in dance is well received by an audience and may give them some indication of the school's dance standard. And so while a theme needs to be family appropriate it also needs to reflect the dancers' need to perform, drawing attention to their particular talents.

Significantly, teachers generally enjoy a close relationship with pupils. They are at the coal face which gives them direct access to the ambitions and ideas of the students. From this position, teachers are able to make use of the ideas that their pupils suggest. The opinions expressed by young pupils are very apt to reflect current trends and elements of youth culture. Utilising the ideas of young people helps to keep material relevant, fresh and inclusive. Some of these processes may delay the theme devising process, but they can provide the foundation for a concerted production with a less risky outcome.

General Themes

Schools that offer a range of dance styles face particular challenges. They need to produce a recital that successfully amalgamates all of the varying dance styles that the school has to offer in a performance .When a dance school has classes as varying as break-dance, tap and ballet, a theme such as 21st century dance, or Summer in the city, gives all dance styles the capacity to collaborate together successfully without undermining the intrinsic characteristics of each dance style and the teachers' choreographic capabilities. General themes allow greater space for stylistic and choreographic interpretation and allow everybody to fully participate on their own artistic terms and merit. A generic theme is less restrictive, more inclusive and affords greater diversity for the stage. However it should be noted that the employment of a less restrictive, all-inclusive theme does have its disadvantages. It should be noted that the employment of a general theme risks a less cohesive production. The many differing components in style, music, dance and setting can lead to a rather cacophonous product in the final analysis.   To avoid this, all parties involved in utilising a general theme should pay greater attention to the choreographic harmony of all components. The work should be monitored as it progresses and the teaching staff should liaise frequently to ensure that everybody continues to sing from the same hymn sheet. In this way you can reduce the chances of   a school producing an incoherent, disjointed dance production at the end of the school year.

Suggested general theme ideas

The four seasons
Summer fever
Winter snow
Snowflakes
Autumn leaves
Spring loaded
The garden at night
21st Century Dance
Disney
Once upon a time
Bach and Beethoven
Bollywood
The fairground
The toy shop
Classical composers
Musicals
The seas
Dance through the ages
Fantasy fairground
Wake Up!
Dance mania
Rock n roll
Dance divas

Dare to dance
Pirates and pixies
Fosse
The sugar plum fairy
The circus
Shirley Bassey
Christmas
Christmas carols
Ghosts and ghouls
The Beatles
The swinging sixties
Party time
Bugs and butterflies
Creatures great and small
The roaring 20s
Dancing through time
Jazz greats
Folksongs
Fairy tales
My favourite things
Under the stars
Fame
Legends and superstars
Michael Jackson
On Broadway
Fantasy
Shirley Temple
So you think you can dance
Superheroes
Summer madness
Carnival
Elvis

Specific themes

A specific theme involves a singular idea that is shared by all parties contributing to a dance recital. The interpretation of the theme is limited, aiming to present a coherent visual picture. Aspects of traditional stories may be selected as a foundation rather than working with the whole narrative. Snow White's poisonous apple may serve as the basis for a whole show rather than utilising the entire tale. The long sleep of Sleeping Beauty may be more interesting to choreograph than the whole notion of her being awakened by a handsome prince. Most often the concept is easily identifiable but is not restricted to pure narrative.

This method is well adapted to schools that are characterised by a specific dance style. Ballet is characterised by its elegant dance quality epitomised by the ethereal ballerina. This dance style is well suited to the fables of yesteryear and is well-known for its use of traditional tales. . It is not uncommon for jazz dance schools to make use of the songs of Louis Armstrong or the work of Bob Fosse. Given the contributions that both these artists have made to the world of jazz, it is fitting that jazz schools are apt to pay tribute to them both.

The contributors of a specific dance recital production are stylistically unified. This includes choreographic material, costumes, music, props and lighting. All parties work in concert to bring to life one concept. Larger studios with a broad dance programme are not excluded from working with a specific theme but there may be some challenges. With the extensive range of dance styles often operating out of a large school, the quest for visual and artistic harmony may be harder to achieve. Different dance styles have different connotations visually, musically and historically. Whilst every attempt may be made to unify all the varying types of dance, the need to integrate costumes, music, props and scenography may render the dance recital more general rather than specific.

Specific theme ideas

Cinderella
Sleeping Beauty
Little Red riding Hood
Frozen
Romeo and Juliet
Richard III
In the Night Garden
Peppa Pig

Grease
Westside Story
42nd street
The elves and the shoemaker
Saturday Night Fever
the Wizard of Oz
Alice in Wonderland
Jungle Book
Lion King
Rapunzel
The princess and the pea
Mary Poppins
Snow White
Oliver Twist
Willy Wonka and the Chocolate Factory

Narrative Themes

A specific theme is particularly successful when mediated through the narrative genre. The audience is captivated by the story at the inception and they are borne along to the story's conclusion. *Westside Story* takes the audience on a romantic journey of love but culminates in devastating consequences. Kenneth Macmillan's *The Invitation* is gripping from the inception and takes the audience along a journey suffused with sexual tension and violence. Unquestionably a dance narrative can compel the attention of an audience.

A narrative theme can cope with a range of class levels, age groups, abilities and experience. A theme entitled The Christmas Present might be broken down into the following segments:

1. Dressing the Christmas tree
2. Placing presents under the tree
3. The night before
4. Christmas morning
5. Christmas lunch with an extended family
6. Opening presents
7. Evening visitors
8. Bidding friends and family goodbye
9. Going to bed

The content of this theme could be approached in many ways. Each segment should have its own sequence of events that contribute to the overall denouement of the narrative. Each section should be choreographically relevant and flow from one scene to the next. The audience should have a clear understanding of each scenario and each setting should preface the next. Choice of music should reflect the seasonal and/or religious setting. The scenes move seamlessly from one set to another.   Each stage set may be slightly adjusted to add visual stimuli and variety.   The scenes may be divided into three sections creating an Act1, Act2 and Act3 for extra gravitas and organisation of material.

Abstract themes

A dance theme could be approached through abstract form. This is a far more amorphous structure with an infinite range of nuances and interpretations. An abstract theme is devoid of all literal ideas, representations and cultural references. Employing an abstract theme can be an exciting exploration into the unknown. There are limitless choices of music, dance, staging and costume. Its non-representational character is a blank canvass where the title theme is the stimulus for creativity. From here, the range of constructs are restricted only by the choreographer's imagination. Overt direction is minimal and exploration into the unknown is what makes this type of theme for some the most creative.

This type of recital might be better suited to a mature dance audience. Given that a dance recital is on the whole a family affair, an abstract dance work may alienate younger viewers who cannot relate to the nebulous intricacies associated with abstract dance. An annual dance recital is better received if it is family friendly, providing entertainment for all of its viewers irrespective of age and dance knowledge.

Abstract themes

Pathways
Aftershock
Variations on a theme
Elements of movement
Infinity
Time
Slow motion
Rebound
Reverberation
Circular motion
Flow
Backfired
Bat and ball
Release
Contract

Points in space
Question and response
Create
Elevation
Ripples
Canon
Dance in Technicolor
Sky's the limit
Blind spot
Black ice
Forward stride
Ricochet
Crystallise
Movement and motif
Construction
In flight
Speed
Parallel universe
Wind
Undulation

Production themes

A themed production refers to use of well-established fables, musicals, tales and other narratives. This could take the form of children's stories such as Little Red Riding Hood, Cinderella and Sleeping Beauty. Equally, the works of Shakespeare, Disney and Westside Story could be used. These stories are choreographically re-created with varying degrees of loyalty to the original script. If produced well, these shows are frequently successful because they are known, loved and can engender nostalgic childhood memories. Unless the work is a modern adaptation, audience members will more than likely have preconceived ideas as to how the work will look overall. These productions are similar to specific themes in that they follow a series of episodic scenes based mostly on the chapters in the selected tale. Modern adaptations provide a fertile ground for large schools. The contemporary version of a traditional tale allows for a much wider remit of ideas, and as such is better suited to schools that are multidisciplinary and offer a range of dance styles. They are free to select from a range of songs that can elicit different elements of the theme. *Come fly with me* by Frank Sinatra could be used for Peter Pan or for The Snowman. *Who let the dogs out* is a good option for a modern adaptation of 101 Dalmatians. Drawing from a range of different music genres in this way renders the production, fun, eclectic and slightly idiosyncratic.

Dance styles from the street dance or hip hop genres respond well to modern adaptations. This has been consistently demonstrated by hip hop dance schools and companies over time. Often, the main theme characterising a tale is used as the foundation for the work. Cinderella may be entitled Rags to Riches. Romeo and Juliet may be interpreted as Love in the Hood. The Prince and the Pauper could be Bruvvas (brothers) across the divide. This production type is very attractive to a younger audience because the content style is familiar. These types of dance productions are often used to make literary genres such as Shakespeare or Chaucer more accessible.

Decisions to not use a theme.

The decision to use a theme for an end of year recital is not obligatory. A school may decide to make use of all the dance routines learned over a year and stage them as a representation of the school's artistic accomplishments. The material may be organised in terms of genre, level or age. However, with this artistic decision it could be argued that a theme does still exist; the theme might be characterised as classwork. The decision to utilise term material is wholly acceptable as long as the work is stimulating and of visual interest. However there are some distinct issues associated with this option. Issues of monotony and chronological fluency loom large. Several classes covering the same syllabus can make for a rather tedious show if the material is not reworked. In addition the routine and repetition used to improve dance technique in class may lack choreographic invention leading to a lacklustre show. But with a considered approach, and a good crop of dances with interesting choreography this option could work just as well as any other. This concept works better if dance recital material is integrated into the planning of class material at the beginning of term or academic year.

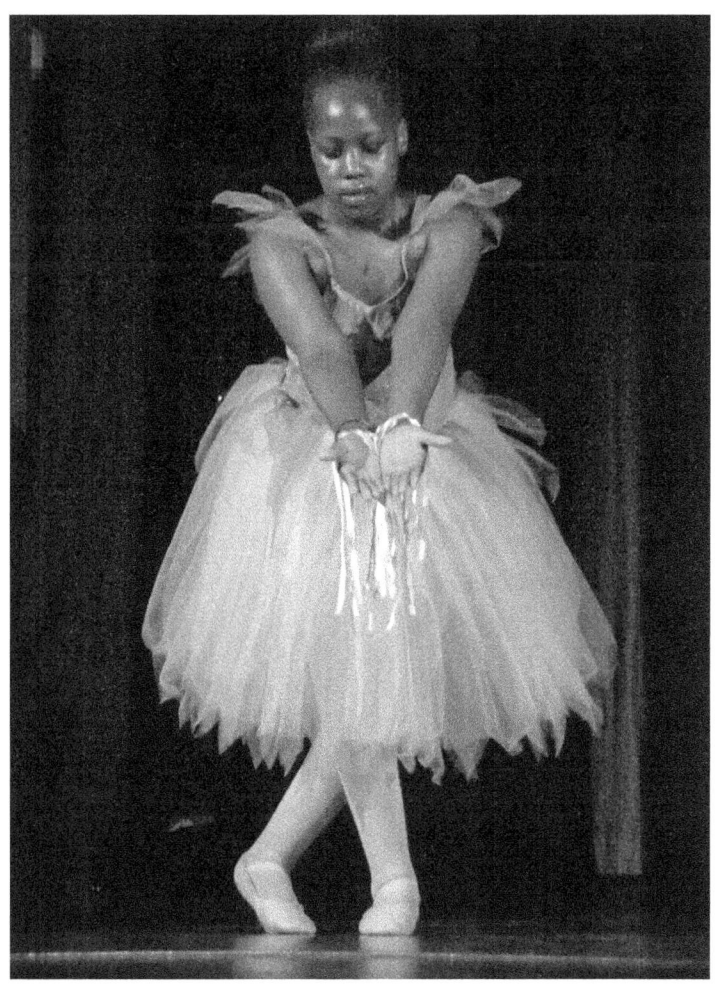

Teaching Recital Material

The end of year recital should be followed by a nurturing period of reflection. This is to review the elements that worked well in the show and critically assess those that were not so successful. It is also a time to look at the interaction of all who contributed to the development of the dance recital. Were the working relationships productive and healthy, or could strategies have been put in place to illicit a better working environment for all involved? It is a time to critically review all areas of the recital. It is a time to compare and contrast the recital the year before and assess whether the most recent show was an improvement on the last. This process is a necessary, cathartic undertaking for the betterment of the dance school, its teachers, and pupils.

Once this period of deliberation is complete, it is time to delve into the creative processes all over again for the next recital. This may seem perhaps a little premature, but just like the time of reflection the next production is an embryonic process that needs time to develop; intellectually first, and then manifest itself choreographically thereafter. It takes time and many changes may take place before the final concept is established.

Once the new term begins, not a moment is to be lost in the dance studio. As much choreographic material should be prepared in advance of arriving in the studio. For some teachers the choreographic process requires periods of spontaneous devising in the studio with dance pupils in attendance. It is one of the techniques often associated with building dance content for performance. For some, studio devising is a key feature in the choreographic process. But if pupils are required to be instrumental in the choreographic process, devising should still be set as part of class planning. Pupils should never be left idle as the teacher tries to prepare material in valuable class time. This is a waste of valuable class time and can cause pupils to lose confidence in the teacher's abilities.   Time management and planning are essential skills that help to facilitate the creation of a dance concert. Use of these skills can avoid many of the problems that manifest closer to the time of the actual dance recital. Pre performance rehearsal cramming can be reduced if not eliminated completely if studio time is managed efficiently throughout the year. Stress and anxiety often associated with the dance recital can also be reduced if time is well managed throughout the year. The aim is to maximise effective use of the time spent with pupils, and to prepare them for performance in a consistently progressive fashion that builds content and confidence to perform.

There should be a dance recital component in every dance lesson throughout the year. This is sometimes a challenge because the yearly exams need to be featured in each class too. But it is important to have pupils performing who are so confident and so well prepared that they are eagerly looking forward to the show, and not intimidated by the whole process.

Teaching very young children requires an extreme amount of repetition. You may be working with children who have yet to become familiar with counts, phrases and spacing. This will all need to be considered when preparing material. You may need to look for music that facilitates children's movement response. Many pre-school action songs dictate the movements to be performed by children. This is achieved by composers creating music that has strong, dynamic contrasting beats that children respond to. This can be very helpful when working with 3-4 year olds. Alternatively, songs that have movement directions integrated into the music are a good option for pre-school children and can help with the choreographic process immensely. Avoid at all costs teaching choreography by counting phrases; toddlers will lose interest. Make funny sounds that mimic the musical rhythms of the movement, clap, and sing the rhythms; anything that makes learning choreography fun. That said, with all the preparation and teaching methods used, little children will always make errors, find themselves in the wrong place, and prefer to stand still and look at their costumes or wave to parents in the audience. With some groups teachers prompt the children from the wings, others go on stage to reposition the children repeatedly. Some schools may utilise dance assistants on stage to help little children perform. Errors on stage can be expected for sure but their performance will still be ever endearing to the audience.

Each week or perhaps every two weeks teach new material in a choreographically developmental structure. Sometimes it is tempting to spend an inordinate amount of time on one choreographic phrase. This is usually because a teacher may feel that the pupils are not quite performing the work as conceived. The teacher may try over and over again to get it performed as originally expected. This should be resisted; move on developing the material progressively. Always have the performance in the forefront of your mind. Better to have the choreography taught and insert additional rehearsals nearer the show than to teach the choreography from scratch just before the show. The latter is a breeding ground for anxiety and stress. Concerns about getting the work completed will start to flourish amongst dancers and parents. Even worse, anxiety may tempt some to pull out of the show altogether for fear of being party to an embarrassing, incomplete production.

Once the material has been taught, children can practise at home. Parents can be given special homework tasks to ensure children practise and subsequently improve on areas where they are weak. Videos of the work can be given to children and parents to work with at home. This will give children and parents the opportunity to practise and spend more time on the choreography than they ever could in class time alone. It is important to encourage home practice several times a week to increase choreographic competence. Practice at home will also test the pupil's ability to perform the work without the aid of others in class. Pupils often rely on their peers to assist in learning dance material. This should be discouraged and pupils should be trained to become independent learners. Home practice is a great supplement to studio work. It encourages pupils to become actively engaged in their own learning and will make your studio work ever more manageable. This will reduce the panic of not getting performance work completed in time for the recital and the learning process will be more enjoyable for all concerned.

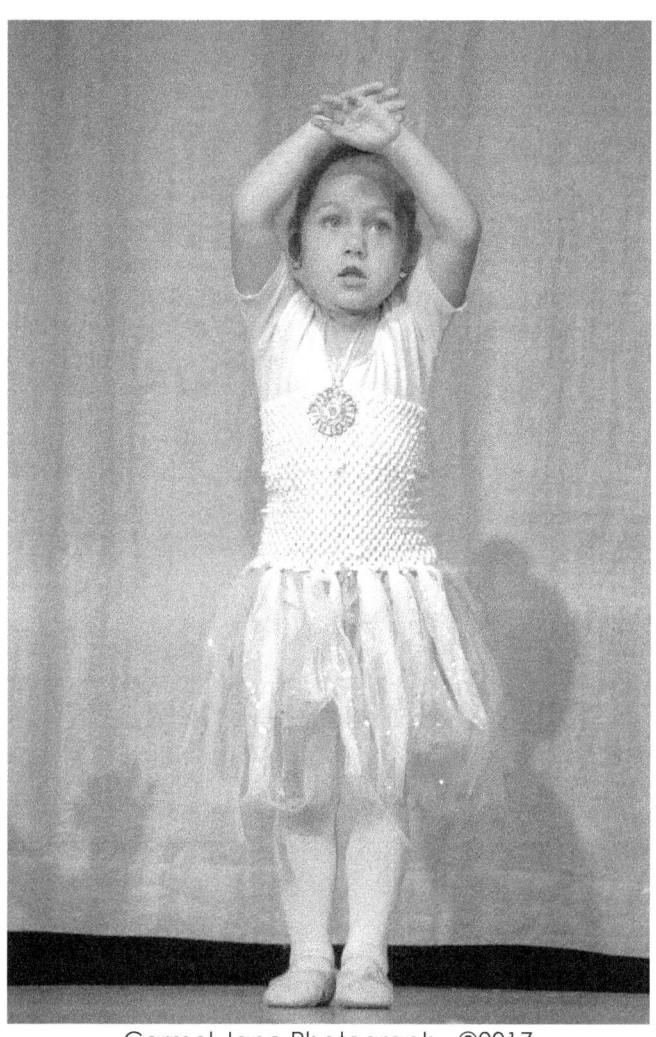

Carmel Jane Photography ©2017

Preparing young children for performance

Preparing the very young to perform can be an intimidating task. Their age and lack of experience makes them vulnerable on stage. There are numerous social media videos vividly demonstrating all the potential pitfalls. Videos show children staring blankly on stage frozen with fear. Other videos show children oblivious to the show and the audience, happily absorbed in their own little universe. But it need not necessarily be like that. Children are more than capable of learning age appropriate dance routines. They can enter and exit stage completely unaided if appropriately prepared.

One of the crucial ingredients to a successful child performance is early planning; another is repetition. A class where the content is predictable is very attractive to children and makes them more responsive. Children enjoy demonstrating what they have learned; even more so where those watching are clearly attentive. Repetition for a child represents familiarity, stability and subsequent security in the material. It is through recurrence that a child learns how to perform actions with confidence. The more familiar an action is, the more proficient a child becomes in that action and the more likely they are to enjoy performing it. The method of repetition engenders confidence and prepares the child for performance. This process should be integrated into the planning stage. The earlier this process is started the more successful the outcome will be.

Choreographing the entrance onto stage is a simple method that will enhance the professionalism of a child dance recital. Often online videos show teachers or helpers chaperoning little ones onto stage. They are taken to their allocated spots on stage in the hope that the children will perform when the music starts. This is all so unnecessary. A simple musical introduction with choreography that has been rehearsed in class will eliminate the need for back stage staff entering with the little performers on stage. The music acts as a trigger for the children and will prompt them to enter the stage totally unaided. This can also be used to set spacing on stage. If the entrance component of a dance is not prepared the chances are that once on stage the children will huddle together unfamiliar with the need to space themselves out across the stage. The need for a backstage chaperone will then be required to enter the stage to reposition the children before the music starts.

 Preparing children to perform independently is a progressive process. As soon as children start attending classes it is wise to equip them with placement spots. These can be as large as mats to start off with if that is all that is available. However be warned that little ones are likely to be distracted by mats. They will enjoy shifting the mats around, looking underneath them and trying to envelope the mats around themselves for fun. But the aim is to gradually decrease the size of the placement mats over time. Sometimes little ones will battle and become possessive of their spacing spots. This can be overcome by declining to issue the same spot to each child every lesson, and to mix it up regularly. But if you are preparing for a particular formation dance, it would be wise to set structure at the inception to avoid the need to restructure at a later stage. Where there are groups of a fair size ensure that the children are aware of "staggering. This could be incorporated into the lesson structure as a game using musical statues as the basis. Fundamentally each child should be able to know the difference between a dancer standing in front of them, and the space directly between two dancers who are standing directly in front of them. Placement spots can be very helpful to assist the children in learning these spatial structures.

Eventually a tiny cross made with masking tape will be all that is needed to guide children to stand in the correct space. This could also be tiny spots, coloured stickers or any other discrete method to lead children to the correct place on stage. If this method is utilised over a few class terms, there will be no need for children to be led onto stage, compromising the professionalism of the recital performance. For several groups performing on stage, colour code or number each position so children are able to identify with ease where they should stand. Some groups may have no need at all for spots such is the success of this method.

It is highly recommended that exit triggers are also used, limiting the "lost child" syndrome at the end of a dance routine. Use of a little outro music or some significant sound towards the end of a dance will dramatically improve the ways in which children exit the stage. Practice the exit as part of learning recital choreography in class on a regular basis to ensure a well-rehearsed exit route. By the time the dress rehearsals and costume fittings have been scheduled, little children will be more than ready with their dance work. Once children are actually performing on stage as part of a recital, a familiar friendly face should be waiting in the wings to direct the children back to the changing rooms afterwards.

Early planning, consistency and repetition will serve the dance recital well. This is particularly important when very young children are performing. For some covering dance studio mirrors in class before a recital may help the preparation process to the theatre. Some schools opt to practice material facing away from the dance studio mirrors. This option is not recommended. To have little ones face the back of the studio for performance practice can be disorientating for older performers let alone children. They lose sight of where to enter, where to exit and often turn back to face the mirror where they feel comfortable. Creating a small audience in class for children to practise performing in front of can provide invaluable experience for children. It is a simple way to familiarise children with the ambience associated with performing.

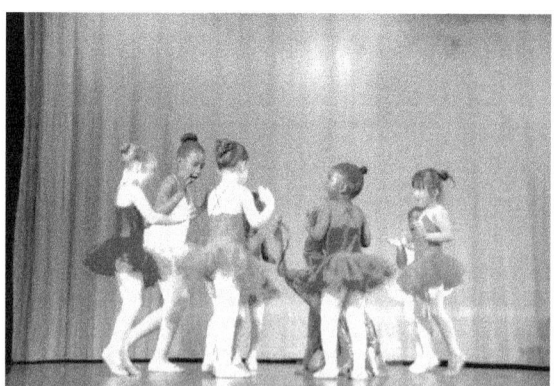

Carmel Jane Photography ©2017

How much content can be taught?

Most children are excited by a dance school recital. They look forward to mums, dads and other family members coming to see them perform. Most will happily accept the sequences given to them and are keen to please. But how much material should they be expected to take on? Depending on the size of the dance school one or two dance routine per class is the norm. This is normally sufficient to meet the requirements of a dance performance of medium length.

For smaller dance schools, a greater burden of work is bestowed upon the upper years. Usually, they are more experienced, more capable and able to carry a greater choreographic load. Conversely each pre-school class   learns fewer dances and they usually form the opening of a recital. The remainder of the show is performed by the rest of the school thereafter. Alternatively, pre-school dance routines are interwoven throughout the entirety of the show. They may play the role of an endearing divertissement or have a pertinent role to play in the recital theme.   It is not uncommon for older groups to perform three or four pieces. The dances performed by the upper years may include group dances, solos and duets. They give the school the opportunity to showcase individual talents and skills. They may also provide the viewer with the opportunity to critically assess the comparative levels of improvement from one year to the next.

But dance recitals are often subject to a rather distasteful reputation. Recitals frequently suffer the notorious reputation of presenting repetitive, uninteresting pieces that are performed for far longer than necessary. This is particularly the case where schools offer numerous classes for children ranging from 2 -3 years. It is therefore sometimes a challenge to keep the choreography fresh and interesting for audience members. Two and three year olds in particular are limited to a very basic vocabulary of movement which may cause a toddler filled recital to suffer endless hours of choreographic repetition. Classes with children ranging from May 3-5 suffer similar choreographic challenges but to a lesser extent. Under these circumstances it is advisable to avoid exceeding a two hour dance recital. It is far better to stage a short, well-conceived recital than one inundated with hours of endless simple dance routines.

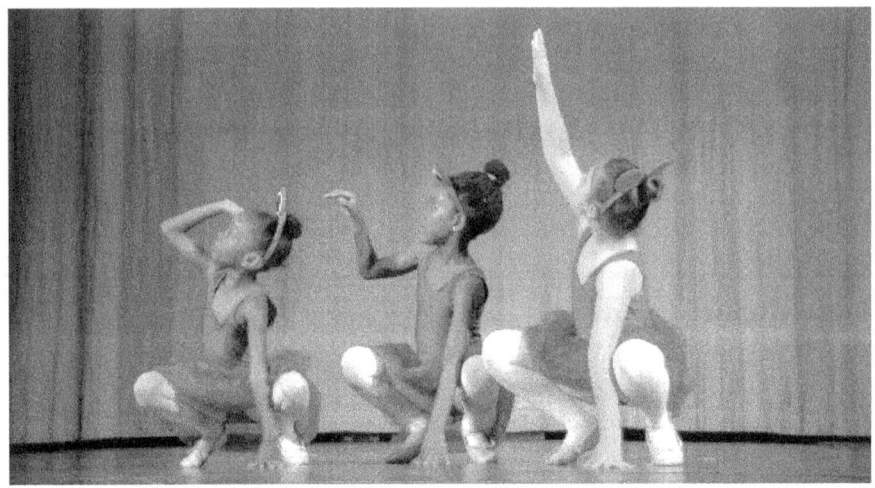

Carmel Jane Photography ©2017

Lighting the stage

Use of effective lighting and stunning backdrops can add a significant difference to a dance recital. Unfortunately these areas are often neglected by schools with much of the work being left to the imagination of lighting technicians. But given time and consideration lighting can have a tremendous effect on a dance production.

Lighting is such a flexible component of a dance performance and its use should be a key feature in any dance concert. It can enhance the narrative being depicted through the movement on stage and hide much of the necessary scene changes required in a dance performance. The absence of lighting i.e. blackout can be used discretely to change scenes concealing the technical shift of props and performers on stage. Similarly blackout can be used to shift the audience's attention to specific dancers on stage and then switch back at the appropriate time. This use of lighting can be utilised to depict opposing groups, disharmony and rivalry. The contrast of light and dark can create stunning movements in silhouette creating a portrait of unimpeded motion in space. In conjunction with the various parts of the stage, such lighting can control the audience's focus of attention and the ways that a narrative is portrayed.

The use of lighting can be used to control the perspective of dance and how it is viewed by the audience. Lighting significantly influences the way a dancer's movement is viewed, the colour of the dancer's skin, the colour of costumes and the overall ambience of a dance. In order to exploit the benefits of lighting, it is necessary to dedicate some time to speak with the lighting technician. Discussions will revolve around the general themes and ideas that characterise the recital, and the ways in which colour can enhance choreography as it hits the stage. A fiery, energetic dance may benefit from powerful red lights, but a peaceful garden setting may be depicted by a cyclorama shaded with a cool green.

The choice of lighting available is dependent on the theatre selected for the dance recital. Some theatres will have a manually operated lighting board whereas others may be computerised. The latter can be programmed requiring the minimal of effort once set up, whereas the former will require a technician to manually execute each change of lighting during the performance via a lighting board. Most theatres will have their own in house lighting technician. They will be very familiar with the lighting facilities and the lights the theatre has to offer. They will also be able to advise of any additional lighting equipment that may be needed for performance. A lighting designer can be hired to work exclusively on a specific dance production. But whichever is chosen, the technician will need to have a working knowledge of the show.

A hired lighting designer may be free to attend rehearsals to see the work in progress as well as attend scheduled studio meetings. He/she will be able to offer advice to teachers and choreographers on how to maximise the effect of choreography on stage. But between the choreographer and lighting technician an agreed schedule of lighting cues must be arranged as a complement to the choreography that is set for performance. This will need to be crafted with the music and the exact times the lighting cues need to be implemented onstage. The clearer the vision of a choreographer, the easier the work is for the lighting designer. He/she will want to add as much value as possible to the recital programme. Will the lights slowly fade from one to another or will they change dramatically from one set to another? Should the lighting form a subtle counterbalance to the choreography or will its role be to add drama? Additional time may be needed to experiment and test a range of effects to establish which lighting effects work best for the dance recital.

In all events lighting adds character and vibrancy, and is an effective visual stimulant for audience members. The lighting component of a dance recital should be included in the recital budget. A cheap, but out of date theatre may require a privately hired lighting designer with a raft of additional equipment needed for a show. A modern theatre may have up to-date facilities but a school may incur a catalogue of unanticipated charges. These could range from additional hourly rates included for meetings with the in-house lighting designer with extra charges based on design complexity. There may be miscellaneous charges for things such as the gaffer tape used on stage and compulsory in-house ticket production. Schools may not be permitted to source their own front of house staff and be required to pay for the in house theatre ushers. There may also be heavy penalties for failing to exit the premises at the agreed time.

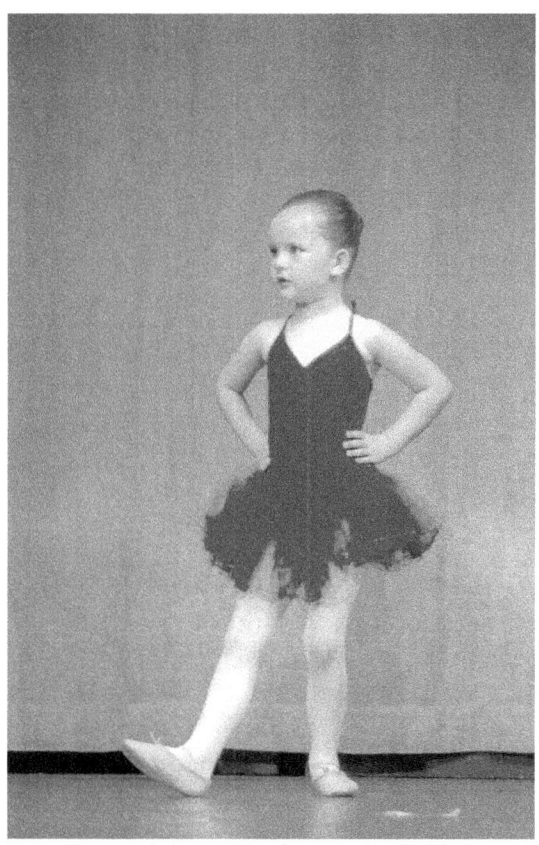

Carmel Jane Photography ©2017

Stage Costumes

Costumes are an extremely important component of the dance recital; they provide additional information about each dance and are visually stimulating to the eye. The use of costume can help create characters that audience members can readily identify and show character development by subtle (or not so subtle) changes in costume. In the beginning, Maria in West Side story is clad in virginal white with a touch of red. But towards the end her red dress represents the loss of innocence and a transition into womanhood. Costumes help the audience to establish the period and location for dance. For instance the costumes in Grease are unmistakably late 1950s America, during the rock n'roll era. Costumes have the capacity to tell a story and show its development. The transformation of Cinderella as she prepares for the ball is one of the most significant scenes in the ballet. The costumes represent an impoverished domestic who is transformed into a mysterious beauty fit to marry a prince. She is aspirational and the costumes help us to engage in her story. Costumes can also help represent the style of dance and choreography. A flowing dress may help characterise the soft flowing movements of lyrical dance and a tutu symbolises the classical form of ballet. Baggy sweats and trainers are synonymous with hip hop whereas bell bottoms signify jazz.

Costumes can enhance choreography and can at times serve as a crutch. Whether by design or error, some dances are unable to convey with accuracy the choreographic intention without the support of a good costume department. Costumes can help audience members to make sense of the ideas underlying an abstract theme. Even with traditional narrative dance the choice of costume can be pivotal. In most classical ballets mime is the driving force in ballet to push forward its narrative and costume assists in the process. How would the romantic ballet Swan Lake be received without the iconic white tutu and white feather headdress? How splendid would the Firebird be without the associated red hot tutu? Costumes help to identify dances set in a historical period whether it be the romantic period or the swinging sixties in London.

For a young performer, the dance costume epitomises the recital. Costume fittings are exciting and children are thrilled by the transformational effect a costume can have. Costumes can give them an infusion of   self-confidence that can effectively boost their dance performance ability.   The dance uniform is jettisoned and replaced with something glamorous, albeit temporary. Meek and mild pupils mutate and become confident happy performers because of the dance costume and the recital.

Financing the recital costume

The ways in which a recital is costumed depends very much upon the school. There are a variety of methods and each school decides the best way based on need, finance and storage. Traditionally costumes were made by the parents of children attending the dance school. Alternatively a seamstress was employed with the sole purpose of making dance recital costumes once a year. But both of these traditions have comparatively faded in popularity in favour of the ready-made dance costume.

All costumes are purchased or ordered well in advance of a recital. This is done to make allowances for any alterations that may need to be made. Costumes may also need to be returned to suppliers due to order errors or design faults in manufacturing. Schools need to be sure that supplies are able to meet demand for the show and any additional last minute orders. It is not uncommon for new pupils to the school to expect to be in a show even if they have missed most of its preparation. But it makes good business sense to attempt to include these new clients whenever possible. Most likely they will have friends and family members keen to see them perform, and they will all want to purchase recital tickets. It is also sensible to harness the enthusiasm of a new pupil and deposit it on stage in performance; where it wants to be. Of course there will be times where late registrants cannot be inserted into a recital. Last minute inclusions can disrupt choreographic formations and burden existing pupils with the restructuring of dance works. This could impair their performance readiness and confidence to perform. Late entries may struggle to learn choreography quickly and thus perform poorly onstage. But costume availability shouldn't exclude a pupil from performing in a recital. Ensure that costumes purchased are readily available to avoid turning down an enthusiastic rookie performer.

There are schools who charge parents directly for each costume used in a show. These costumes are not kept by the school but are given to the child at the end of the recital. This method is useful if the school does not have space to develop a costume wardrobe. This method can create additional funds for the school as bulk purchases are awarded discounts but parents are charged the normal retail price. But even with this method, any additional items needed-stage props for instance - are purchased and kept by the school. Costumes purchased by parents are sometimes kept for nostalgic reasons, but eventually most are often sold online as second hand goods. Second hand costumes make good purchases as they have been worn for rehearsals and a few shows at the most. Normally they are still in very good condition and can be recycled to be used again.

Other schools charge parents a recital fee. This payment contributes to all things related to the show of which costumes are one. The costumes are kept by the school forming part of a wardrobe department and is used for subsequent performances throughout the year. This recital charge may be integrated into the general term fees over the year or added as a supplement near or during the recital term. This method can be of immense benefit to a school. As the wardrobe develops over time the recital fee can be used towards other areas of the show. This may include employing official chaperones, recital advertising, publicity material and array of other things related to the show.

Another popular choice made by some schools is to charge parents a costume hire fee. These rates are not standardised and are subject to the quality of the costume, its original price, maintenance requirements and the costume size. This latter method can incur additional charges if costumes are kept past an agree date or they are returned damaged. This method does help to reduce the charges that are passed onto parents, but such costumes require space and management throughout the year.

Fundraising for costumes are a popular method for some schools. Once the target budget has been reached, any additional funds may contribute towards things such as term fees, music, theatre trips or anything that the school pupils can benefit from. Some schools give any financial profits to charity.

Before a recital, the costumes are usually given to parents in advance. They are taken home and then the child may arrive in full costume for performance. This reduces the   time parents or recital staff spend back stage preparing children for stage. Parents deliver their children to an appointed person who registers their attendance and then parents promptly leave the theatre. Other schools may require parents to arrive with child and costumes in tow. They go backstage to prepare the children and then leave backstage before the start of the show. It is advisable to notify parents about the importance of looking after costumes and if necessary to return them. Some parents may assume that there is a ready supply of costumes ready to replace damaged or lost ones. If not advised some parents may be quite cavalier about looking after them.   Also if not notified to the contrary some parents will keep costumes as a performance memento.

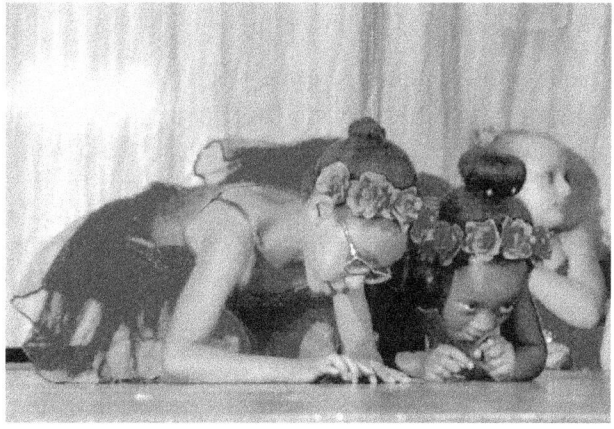
Carmel Jane Photography ©2017

Backstage

For many the prospect of a dance theatre performance is so exciting. So much so that all your back stage organisation can fall to the wayside when parents are unable to resist the temptation to steal a glimpse back stage under the guise of some important task they need to fulfil. Often they are overwhelmed with curiosity and a desire to check that their child is OK and see what is happening. But the presence of a misplaced mum can elevate stress levels that prior to her presence were kept under control. Parents don't always appreciate the pressures back stage and the desperate need to keep things as planned.

Parents are often quite keen to help backstage, but only if it involves preparing their own children alone for performance. Those who make themselves available for overall volunteering are few and far between. It is essential that you treasure these angels in the hope they will proffer their services on a regular basis. Offers of free tickets, flowers, additional private lessons or reduced term fees are incentives for parents to offer their services backstage. Some schools include a volunteer clause for parents to sign at the registration stage of their children starting with the school. This might be successful for some schools but reluctant parents will always find an escape route if need be. It may be helpful to post in advance the number of volunteers needed and the tasks to be performed. Post this information where it is clearly visible for all parents to see. Put up this information a couple of months prior to the recital to give parents the opportunity to reflect before deciding. Once you have the required number of volunteers, you can start arranging staff meetings to discuss their duties and how their individual jobs relate to each other and the recital as a whole.

You will find that in the main the majority of parents simply want to sit back and watch their children perform in the comfort of a paid auditorium seat. This is understandable, especially as many schools do not permit parents to watch classes throughout the term. Staffing dance recitals is a challenging issue for many schools and each school finds a suitable solution, albeit often temporary. It is a good idea to introduce the recital volunteers and chaperones to the parents. For the very young especially, mums are likely to develop concerns for their children if they do not know who is looking after them in their absence. This is exacerbated if the child has any health issues. Wherever possible a quick introduction to parents will go a long way in alleviating anxiety and impromptu visits backstage. The best time for this is in any of the lessons preceding the recital or staff meetings.

For those parents who are happy to help, it is vital that they are given an outline of the held expectations for them. The more detailed this is, the easier it will be for all concerned. Helpers need to know who they are responsible for, including their ages, back stage needs and how their group is integrated into the show. For instance, issues such as costume changes for the very young, toilet visits, and managing backstage boredom will all come under the helper's job description. They need to know where the dressing rooms are - a note on the door is helpful for everybody with the names of all the children located therein. They need to know if the dressing room is shared and know where all the costumes are kept for their charges. They will need to know who the general backstage manager is, and be able to report to her if and when necessary. The backstage manager plays a vital role in integrating all the various groups of the show together. They are on hand to liaise with each volunteer and help solve any pertinent issues in each group. The manager communicates with the lighting and sound technician to design a lighting and sound programme well in advance of the show and discuss any special effects beforehand. She will check the readiness of the stage and make any additional preparations if necessary. Hiring dance floors, extra lighting effects etc. all come under the stage manager's job description. The stage manager often works with the front of house staff including all stewards in small productions.

It is helpful to compile an information sheet that includes the roles of all volunteers and chaperones. This will give all involved a clear picture of how the whole programme is organised and help staff to interact with each other more efficiently. When working with the very young, additional help with toilet visits will need to be organised as this will be a frequent feature backstage. Select one person whose sole responsibility is to chaperone children to and from the bathroom.

Volunteers will need to know when to chaperone the group or individuals towards the wings in preparation for stage entrances. Sometimes a nervous volunteer will bring the group to the wings prematurely in fear of missing their cue. As a result excited little ones can be seen from the auditorium frequently poking their heads out from the wings looking to see if they can locate their families in the audience. In child productions these indiscretions are forgivable if not endearing. If a chaperone is fortunate enough to have a walkie talkie, this process is far more manageable. Once the pupils are on stage she may also need to stay in the wings to encourage children to leave the stage once they have finished performing. Unless the stage exit has been choreographed into the work, it is very common for little ones to remain on stage appearing a little confused as to what to do next. Once off stage, volunteers need to manage their group until the show has completely finished and the children are set to be returned to their parents. As children are returned volunteers should judiciously sign each child off. The bigger the recital is, the more children there are, the more important these processes become.

In order to ensure that all volunteers are up to speed with their roles, pre-recital meetings should be organised. These meetings should be consolidated with additional means of communication. Experience shows that vital information needs to be repeated on different occasions and in different formats. Emails and messages via various forms of social media are helpful. But even the odd telephone call might also be necessary. It is not uncommon for volunteers to arrive in theatres oblivious of their responsibilities despite all attempts to pre-empt such situations. To avoid this information needs to be disseminated repeatedly to ensure all volunteers have received the relevant information in one format or another. Even if volunteers have recital experience it is always good practice to duplicate information. Tension is very high backstage before a recital and good organisation helps to keep this under control. Everyone wants the recital to run smoothly and effortlessly. For this to happen everyone needs to know and do exactly as required.

It is always helpful to appoint a security guard at a recital. This could be a parent volunteer or an older student. Have the appointed wear a tag that is clearly marked 'security' and have them stand on guard in front of the theatre entrance(s). In addition, give your appointed security guard a list of all those who are permitted backstage and or provide a pass for all persons entitled to be backstage.

Parental Guidelines

The following is a guide of things that parents may need to know in preparing for a dance recital. It is by no means exhaustive but includes some of the vital things parents need to be aware of. Some components may change according to the methods employed by the school. For instance some schools may provide costumes for children whereas others may expect parents to finance all costumes. These differing methods will determine how the costume advice will be managed. Photographers may be replaced with a videographer or both may be in attendance. Some recitals have a complete food restriction backstage, but this will largely depend on the age of the performers and the length of time spent backstage.

IMPORTANT RECITAL: INFORMATION FOR PARENTS

Please ensure that you read this information thoroughly for your convenience and to help the show run smoothly.

Recital Date................

Time............................

Theatre Address..

1. Dress   rehearsals
   Dress Rehearsals are a scheduled time for practice onstage, where your child wears their costume along with correct hair,

tights, shoes and make-up. A dress rehearsal gives the pupils time to get used to the stage, and allows the teacher to make any corrections needed before performance. Please do not miss this. Attendance is mandatory.

2. Backstage
   Please note that parents are not allowed backstage. Only volunteers and other staff members are allowed in the backstage areas. Parents are required to bring their children into the theatre at the designated time and then the children will be taken backstage. Please arrive on time.

3. Recital day
   After you check in your children, you are required to leave the theatre and return at *doors open* time. Once your child is checked in, you will not see her/him until the show is finished. You are kindly asked to leave the theatre and come back at the opening of the show as an audience member.

4. Food
   Please ensure your child has had enough to eat and drink before arriving at the theatre. Please give your child a bottle of water, some fruit, and some non-messy, non-noisy snacks (no nuts). Make sure all snacks are clearly labelled with your child's name. Please do not give your child sweets of any kind or anything with colour that may stain or damage costumes. Please avoid all sticky foods.

5. Down time
   Please give your child, pencils and some paper or a book for down time. Do not give your child a mobile phone or any noisy computer gadgets. Please bag these items in a well labelled bag.

6. Costumes

   All costumes should be put in a sealed bag with your child's name clearly written on it. If you have a zipped hanger please use this. Please ensure that your child's shoes are labelled inside the shoe. Also ensure that you have a change of clothes for your child to leave the theatre in, and a spare pair of tights for the recital. Put these in a labelled bag. Volunteers will make sure your child is changed and ready for each dance onstage. Check that all costumes, head pieces and props items are grouped and packed together.

7. Make-up/ hair

   Please apply light make up. Some pink / red lipstick, blusher, a little subtle toned eye shadow, eyeliner and mascara. This is essential because theatre lights tend to dull the face, giving a washed out look. Please include some make-up in your child's costume bag to touch up just before the show. You are advised to practise your child's hair and make-up in advance of the recital to avoid panicking on the day. Please include extra hair pins, hair nets and elastic bands in your child's bag

8. Bathroom visits

   Please ensure your child has visited the bathroom before arriving at the theatre. It is essential that toilet visits are kept to a minimum during rehearsals.

9. Jewellery

   Please ensure that all jewellery including watches are removed before arriving at the theatre.

10. Picking up your child

    Please ensure you have a change of clothes for your child. Put these in a labelled bag and hand them in when you bring your child. After the show is finished, the children will change back into everyday clothes. One parent per family will collect the children when they are back onstage at the end of the show. Your child will need to be signed off before you leave.

11. Tickets

Please ensure you come to the performance with your tickets as purchased. You will need to purchase them again if you do not have your tickets when you arrive. This may be reimbursed when your tickets have been located.

12. Photography

Before and during the dress rehearsal, there will be a professional photographer who will be taking individual photos of each performer. These photos will be available online after the show for purchasing. Please do not take photos during the recital

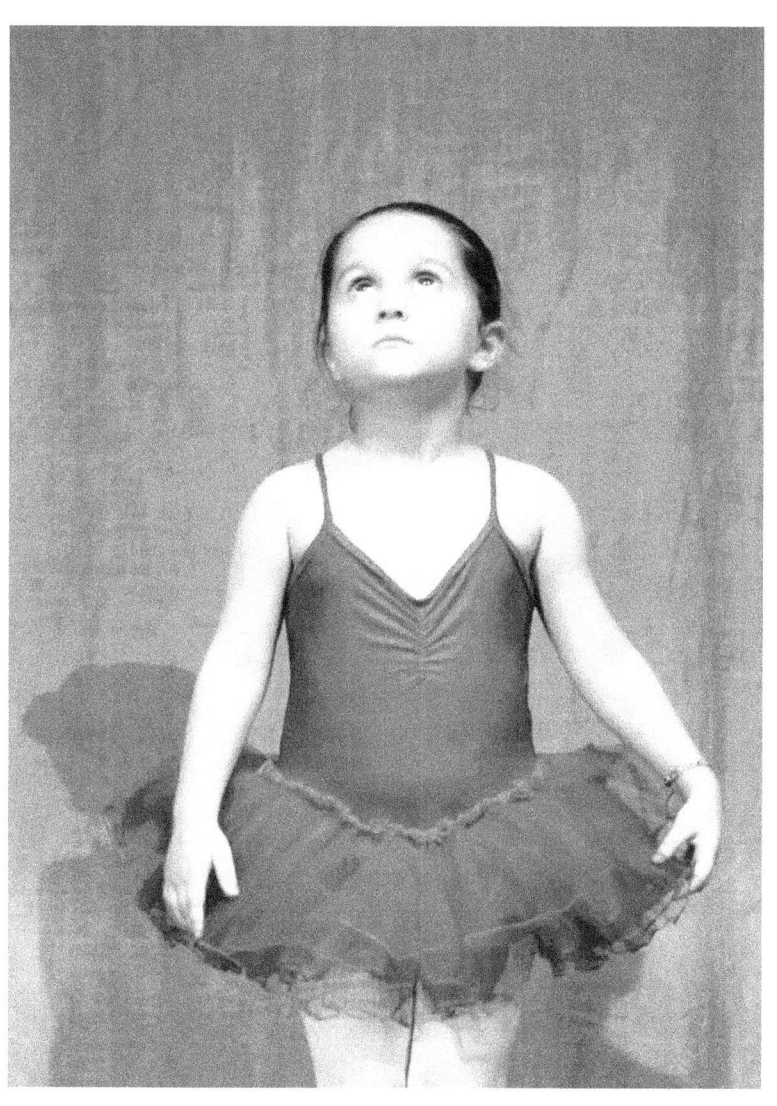

Carmel Jane Photography ©2017

Dance Recital Sign-in Sheet

Recital title:

Chaperone
Name_____Date_____
_____

Student Name	Guardian Name	Guardian Signature	Time In	Time Out	Guardian Signature

The above form is a template for all chaperones with children in their charge. It is reassuring for chaperones to have a formal break down of precisely who they are responsible for and the length of time. It is helpful for them to know when children are signed in and when they are released from their responsibility. The form clearly notates when the guardian signs the child out and takes over guardianship. This safeguards the chaperone against any incidents that may take place after responsibility has been relinquished and notifies the guardian that the child is back under his/her care. Schools may wish to add more data but as it stands the above is simple and fit for purpose

Recital running order template

The template below is designed for distribution to all volunteers and chaperones. It is a basic performance running order that schedules the entire show.   It gives all back stage staff a breakdown of the music, dances, performers and other miscellaneous information regarding the show. It is recommended that this document is given to staff well before dress rehearsals and the recital. This will give them time to read the document, become familiar with its contents and be prepared with any questions at follow up meetings.

When dancers perform in several pieces it is not uncommon for them to switch from one chaperone group to another. This sheet will help chaperones to identify who they need to liaise with to ensure cross over transitions run smoothly without impeding the organisational flow of the performance.

It is important that the form documents all dances in the correct order of the show, as would be the case with a standard running order. Ensure that chaperones can clearly identify all of the dances that his/her group performs in, with additional guidelines as to when they are performed. Providing additional information such as songs and stage directions help chaperones to become familiar with the show as a complete entity. Some chaperones may select to research songs that are unfamiliar to them in preparation for the show. This helps them to know the show by music as well as by sight. This can be very helpful backstage. Similarly they may choose to acquaint themselves with all the performers in their group well in advance to improve the working environment in the theatre.

The sheet includes all aspects of the show including the curtain call, award ceremonies and all on stage activities. The more information given the better prepared back stage staff will be. Once the document has been distributed to all parties ensure all are fully conversant with its contents to avoid unnecessary back stage mishaps.

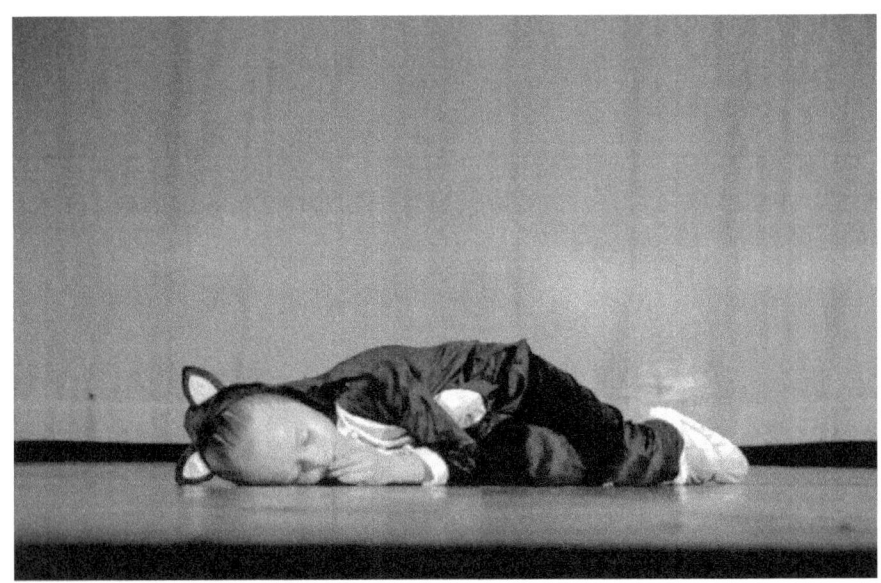

Carmel Jane Photography ©2017

Stage Manager:
Lights up- -/--am/pm

DANCE TITLES	DANCERS	MUSIC	STAGE ENTRANCE/EXIT INFORMATION
Group 1 Room 1 Chaperone: Nancy Lovejoy			
Responsible for: Tom Smith, Sara Moore, Elaine Pinnock, Aisha Clark			
1. Let's All Dance	Tom Smith, Sara Moore, Elaine Pinnock, Aisha Clark	The Gettaways	Enter stage left in black out. Tom Smith remains on stage for solo.
2. Blue Days	Tom Smith	Sleazy Joe	Exit stage right with lights up

Group 2 Room 2 Chaperone:
Responsible for:
  3.

  4.

Group 3 Room 3 Chaperone:
Responsible for:
  5.

Group 4 Room 4 Chaperone:
Responsible for:
  6.

FINALÉ: CAST REMAIN ON STAGE
LIGHTS UP
School Principal Certificate Presentation (in group order)

1st Group	2nd Group	3rd Group	4th Group
Chaperone:	Chaperone:	Chaperone:	Chaperone:
Dancers	Dancers	Dancers	Dancers
1.	1.	1.	1.
2.	2.	2.	2.
3.	3.	3.	3.
4.	4.	4.	4.

School Principal Flowers Presentation (4 persons)
ALL EXIT STAGE LEFT
Children returned to parents by chaperones and signed off in auditorium

ADDITIONAL INFORMATION:

Chaperone support: (general help back stage)
Front of House:
Stewards:

Backstage Ettiquette

To facilitate a happy recital there are some cultural norms that need to be observed backstage. Where to put costumes, space allocation, and noise rules all contribute to a harmonious back stage working environment.

It is customary for performers to identify for themselves a little space or cupboard to place all of their performance paraphernalia. This might just be the empty space under a chair. Once they have established a little plot of their own dancers may use this space for personal props, costumes, makeup, water and perhaps light snacks. All recital participants should be made aware of the necessity to guard their own property and not the property of others. Well meaning pupils have been known to remove costumes and props because they seem abandoned or misplaced. The ramifications of this can be quite devastating. This random act of 'kindness' could compel a dancer to perform without key props or not dance at all because costumes are perceived to be lost. The rates of stress and tension can dramatically increase backstage when a dancer is frantically trying to find her performance attire. Even when the costumes and props are found the pressure of having had to look for them can impact heavily on performance. Equally, if enough costumes are misplaced, the performance could suffer a significant delay. This could incur additional charges to the studio if the recital exceeds the agreed length of time in the theatre. If this isn't enough, working relationships can be impaired and friendships broken. So the rule backstage is that mature dancers should be responsible for their things only. All performers and staff should refrain from repositioning, moving or adjusting anything that they do not own. No matter how peculiar something may appear to be situated, it should be left well alone. What may appear to be a gesture of goodwill could rapidly turn into a fiasco.

Once dancers have reached the age of responsibility they should have a full understanding of the performance running order and know where they should be at all times. A detailed running order should be posted at a convenient location for all to view as a reference. But age permitting, dancers should be fully conversant with the content of a show and know how it relates to their dances. They should have a working knowledge of their stage entrances and exits, and move efficiently from place one to the other without encumbering others. They should not rely on others for information; in essence they should be prepared. They should understand the running order, have their props and costumes placed in an area that is easy to access but does not impede the movement of others. Costumes should be positioned in chronological order to facilitate costume changes throughout the show.

Kids Backstage

When children are young and new to the theatre it is advisable for teachers to spend time teaching them about the norms of the theatre. The subject should be approached in an informal, child friendly manner, making the information part of performance preparation in class time. Young children should be made aware of the darkness in the theatre and how bleeding light from the wings can affect stage lighting and distract the audience. Blackouts in particular should be practised in the studio for the under fives. If need be, the use of a torch may help children learn how to walk towards the wings in the dark. They need to learn that they should only see the audience when they are on stage and not draw attention to themselves by fidgeting in the wings. They need to resist the urge to peer from behind the curtains to view the audience and look for familiar faces. This can be a challenging task. To help young children it might be advisable to demarcate the boundaries between the wings and the stage. They need to practise being quiet, and know the eating policy backstage. This preliminary work should assist back stage staff during performance time. The younger the children are, the more challenging the organisation of backstage is. It is prudent to give children as much preparation and support as possible. The better the preparation is for little ones, the more confidently they will perform on stage when required. Preparation may also help them to feel relaxed when in the theatre.

It is assumed that older dance pupils will be familiar with the norms of backstage. But to be sure that they do, it doesn't harm to revise all salient points with them. That said even if they do understand the practices of backstage they should not busy themselves trying to organise others. To do this could jeopardise their own working schedule. Backstage it is helpful to have a designated person who is responsible for ensuring all performers are ready and prepared . Depending on the number of performers, their age, and the length of the recital there could be several people taking up this post. In most circumstances dancers and their groups will have been given a designated place to stay backstage and they should remain there unless advised to the contrary. Failure to to do this could cause stage cues to be missed and dancers could find themselves in the wrong place at the wrong time. Worse still when dancers move away from their allocated places they may be deemed missing. This conclusion might prompt a stage manager to start the show if the missing dancer cannot be located in time. The stage manager in a school recital may not be a professional but a volunteer who has experience in management. They would liaise with all backstage staff, the theatre staff, dance teachers and relevant studio staff including perhaps the studio owner.

Backstage is often full of nervous tension and excitement. Young adults and children who are often animated by the atmosphere talk endlessly and lose sight of the need to be quiet backstage. Noise in the wings can carry itself into the auditorium making it possible for the audience to be distracted even when the performance is taking place. Children need to be quiet and ignore those who choose not to. That said, theatre rehearsals can be long and tedious especially for children and there are times when dancers are left with nothing to do whatsoever. Perhaps they are waiting for a rehearsal to start or the lighting is yet to be set. To prevent restlessness during these periods of inactivity, advise pupils to bring something to occupy the time. Things that are quiet and small are ideal for inactive times backstage. Encourage reading and colouring books for the very young during downtimes. Computer games may be permitted as long as the sound is muted.

All of these theatre norms form part of the training for young dancers and should be integrated into their dance education from an early age.

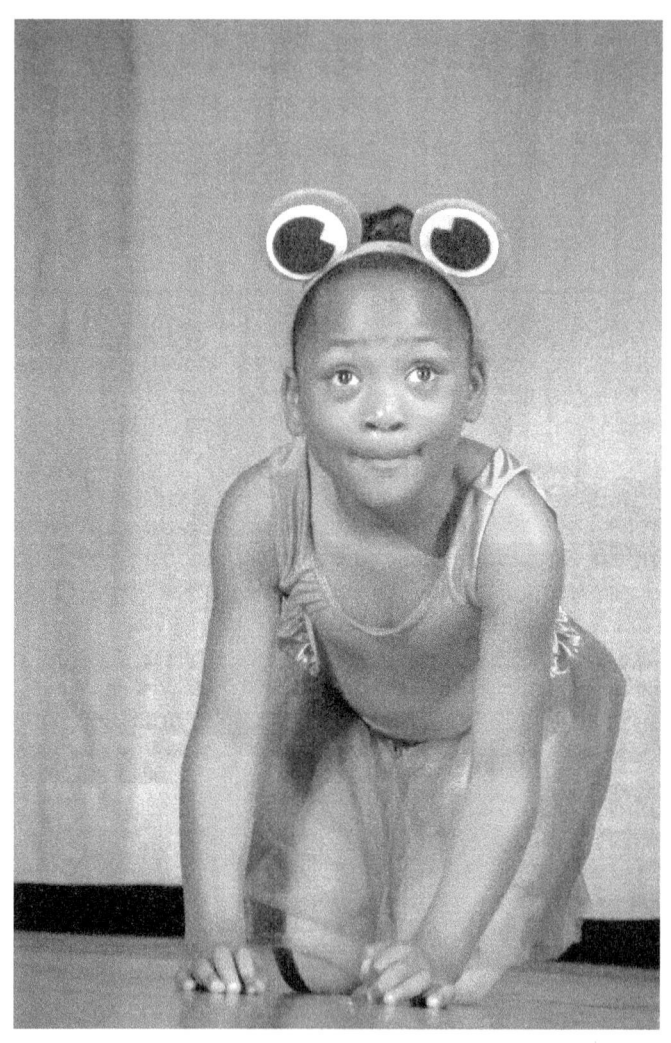

To Licence or not to licence

On 15 December 2014 the Secretary of State for Education passed the Children (Performances and Activities) (England) Regulations 2014.

In the UK a child performance licence is deemed a requirement by law. The law states:

"The licensing authority must impose any conditions which it considers necessary in order to ensure that—

(a) The child is fit to take part in the performance or activity;

(b) Proper provision is made to secure the child's health and kind treatment; and

(c) Proper provision is made to ensure that the child's education will not suffer."

The interpretation of these conditions are subject to regional variations which the law permits. It is felt that local authorities are best placed to make decisions based on the knowledge of groups in their locality. In essence, all performers of school age are required to have a performance licence for performances made in public. A performance licence may be required whether or not a child is paid, and whether or not the performance is professional. Rehearsals taking place during the performance period are subject to the same restrictions and conditions. There are some exemptions to consider.

The four day rule

This rule refers to the permissible number of shows performed by a child each year. If a child has not performed on more than 3 days within 6 months, a licence is not required. But if a performance is during school time, permission from the Head teacher is still normally required.

Educational School Performances

If a child is performing under arrangements made by a school that provides its main statutory education, a licence is not needed. This refers to performances where the school is responsible for organising and producing the show. It is anticipated that such school performances will not infringe upon the legal educational conditions set by the government.

Non School Based Performances

It is at the discretion of the head teacher to permit a leave of absence for a performance scheduled during school hours. Often a head teacher may only authorise absences where a licence has already been obtained for the child. All performing arts schools that do not provide primary or secondary education as part of its provision are required to obtain a licence of some kind when organising performances.

Exemptions for a standard child licence
- The child has not performed for more than three days in the last six months
- No time off from school is necessary to perform
- The child is not remunerated for performance
- The performance is organised by the school

Licenced chaperones

In situations where parents and teachers are not present, chaperones may need to be employed. A child performing or rehearsing for a performance under a licence, must be supervised by an official chaperone at all times whilst taking part. The chaperone will require a licence supplied by the local authority. Chaperone licences are awarded annually and subject to certain criteria. The number of children a chaperone can look after is about twelve. This figure may be adjusted according to the nature of the performance. Each chaperone application is made to the local authority and each chaperone will need clearance by the Disclosure and Barring Service.

Body of Persons approval (BOPA)

An organisation responsible for putting on a performance may apply to the local authority for a BOPA. This is a licence for a specific performance(s) for a limited period of time that permits children to perform. It does not however negate the normal criteria associated with a general child performance licence. It simply grants an organiser the option to gain a licence for a specific event(s) over a prescribed period of time without needing to apply for a licence for each individual child. A BOPA does not authorise absence from school. If the performance involves absence from school, the organisers still require permission from all the schools that the children attend. In certain circumstances a child may be able to attend a performance without school permission. This usually requires an organisation to obtain an ordinary child licence from the local authority where the performance dates have been prescribed.

A BOPA will not be authorised where financial payments are made on behalf of children. A BOPA approved performance does negate the requirement for local authority licenced chaperones. The maximum number of consecutive days a child may perform is six. For a successful application the local authority will seek assurance that the organisation has clear policies for safeguarding children. They will need to be certain the education and health of all children are not compromised and the conditions of the BOPA are observed.

With a warrant the local authority may carry out inspections where rehearsals and performances are taking place. This is to ensure performances and rehearsals are being carried out as defined by council guidelines. Subsequently, local authorities have been awarded powers to revoke performance licences when and where deemed necessary within their jurisdiction. However in most circumstances the intention is to ensure good and safe practice for children. With this in mind they are more likely to work with the dance recital organisers to improve conditions for child performers.

In addition to filling in a form of the type exemplified below, organisers will need to supply information such as the full names and birth dates of each child. Passport identification, birth certificates and passport sized photos may all be required to complete a BOPA. The school each child attends will be required, as well as full information regarding the dates and performance venues. An application for a BOPA cannot be made if children are paid to perform.

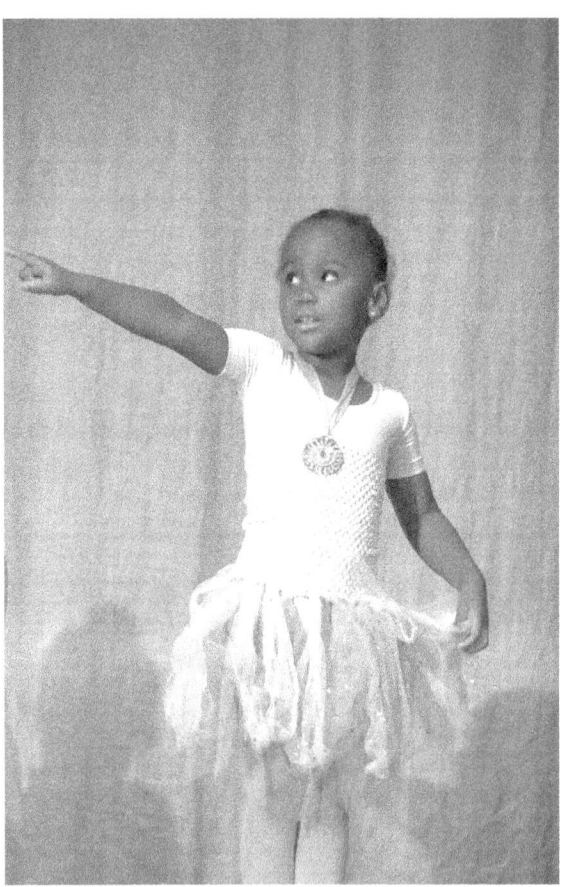

Body of Persons Licence Application form

Name of Production Company	
Name of Applicant	
Position	
Address	
Telephone Number	
Fax Number	Email Address

Performance Title		
Location of Performance (Address)		
Dates of Performance		
Times of Performance		Number of Chaperones per show
Dates of Rehearsal(s)		
Times of Rehearsals		
Place of Rehearsals		

Chaperone Name	Address	Licence Number (If known)	Local Authority

I declare that the above adults are the only adults that will accompany the young people (with the exemption of their parents) they will form this 'Body of Persons'

Signed   Date

Full Name   Position in Company

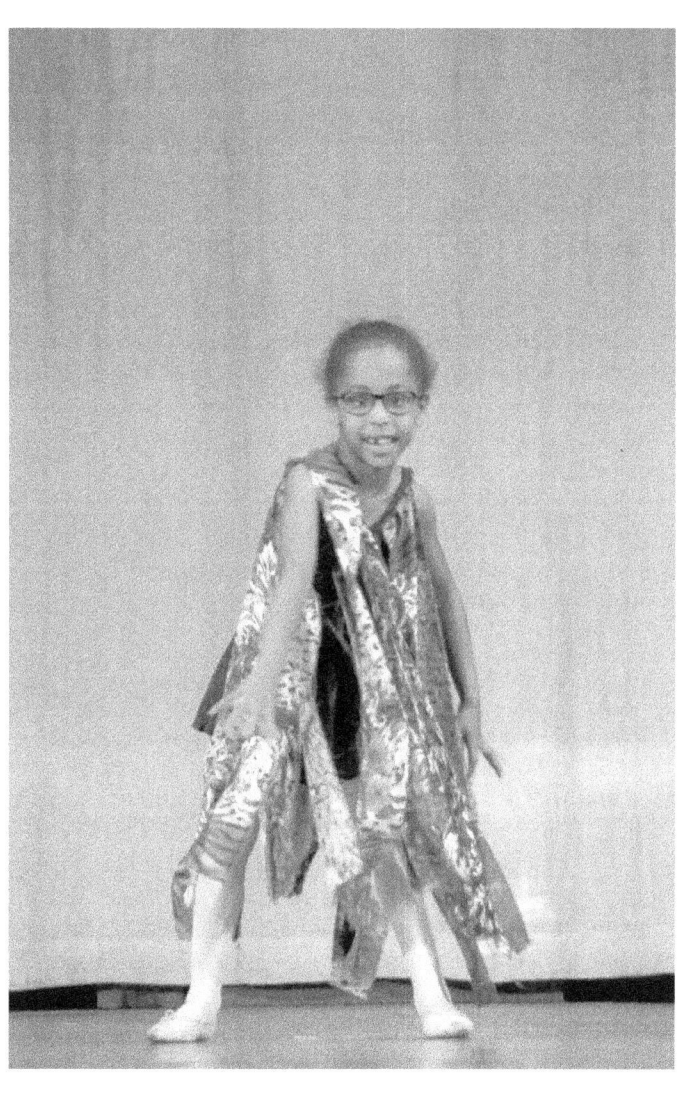

Carmel Jane Photography ©2017

Insurance

A dance school has a duty of care to its recipients like any other business. As such public liability insurance is a must for all dance schools. It protects the school against claims for damages from dance pupils and members of the public. Where multiple teachers are employed, employer liability insurance is equally important and a school is breaking the law if it is employing staff without it.

When a school briefly relocates to a theatre for the end of year recital, some schools may assume that they are adequately insured during this time. They may erroneously assume that their normal insurance policy will stretch outside the boundaries of the dance school environment. This is not necessarily always the case. It is imperative that the details of an insurance policy is checked to see whether its remit stretches further than the dance school perimeter. Even when insurance policies cover theatre shows, there may be limitations as to what is precisely being covered. For instance, a policy for general dance cover may not cover dance works that include acrobatic tricks. Where acrobatics are covered perhaps aerial tricks are restricted.

It is possible to get additional insurance cover on an existing policy on a temporary basis to include a dance performance. But a policy that does not permit off site events would require a school to seek special events cover for a dance recital. This is the best option where an insurance policy is limited. But even with this type of insurance there are other pending issues to consider. Issues such as the number of performances being held, its time frame and location will impact on the type of insurance available. Other issues such as the number of performers, the ages of performers, and a school's safeguarding policies may determine a school's eligibility for additional insurance cover.

Dance event Insurance can cover other areas such as equipment, which can include costumes, props, and merchandise and box office receipts. Thankfully it is also able to cover impromptu cancellations, extreme weather and loss of revenue. Most insurance companies are able to provide standard dance studio cover but it is advised to take up insurance with a company that has a proven record of insuring dance schools, events and dance teachers for peace of mind. Some professional dance societies have internal insurance policies that have been designed expressly for their members. This   is a useful set-up as a dance society is fully aware of its associates' needs and is able to tailor the insurance to meet their special requirements.

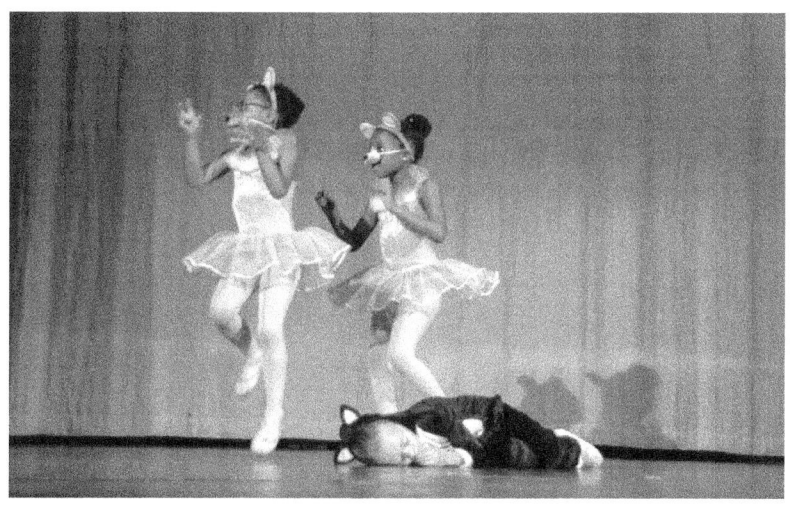

Carmel Jane Photography ©2017

Performing Rights Society

The Performing Right Society (PRS) are a UK established monitoring organisation that seeks to protect the work of all artists who are registered members. They work to make certain that artists are paid in the form of royalties for the music that is used in theatres, dance studios and any kind of public building.

In order for music to be played publicly in the UK permission in the form of a licence is necessary. This licence is granted by PRS who may issue it monthly, quarterly, annually or on an event specific basis. All theatres are required to obtain a PRS licence and upon doing so will entitle all artists who perform there to use the music of artists who are PRS members. A theatre staff member is required to collect the details of all songs used throughout the licence period and submit this information to PRS. The theatre is duly charged for the use of the songs of which an amount is paid directly to the artists.

Music in theatres

While it is a legal requirement for theatres to obtain a PRS licence, artists are not obliged to join. PRS is merely an organisation that systematically collects royalties for artists who elect to join the company. However artists who are not protected by PRS leave themselves open to having their music used with no official body to act on their behalf. In such circumstances the onus will be upon the artists themselves to address unauthorised use of their music. Where artists are not subscribed to PRS it is courteous for them to be contacted directly for a request to be made to use their material.

It is not uncommon for dance events to be cancelled due to PRS taking swift action on behalf of its members. The onus is upon the theatre to submit accurate details regarding the use of music and its authors. Where theatres have been found to be negligent they may be subject to heavy financial penalties. But theatres are also dependent upon schools to provide the correct information when staging recitals. PRS inspectors spend much of their time looking for performances where unauthorised music is being played. This is done by browsing through social media sites, general advertising and online websites. It is a common complaint that PRS employ cold call methods to many organisations in the attempt to investigate unauthorised use of music. They are also known to make clandestine theatre visits to check that music is being used as indicated or otherwise.

Musical theatre and PRS

In addition to the use of music PRS seeks to protect the copyright of musical theatre productions. Well known musical theatre productions are a popular feature of dance recitals but additional care must be taken not to trespass upon copyright conditions. Whilst dance schools may be free to use the music of famous musical theatre productions, care must be afforded with every choreographed step. At no point must the content of a dance recital bear resemblance to the work of the original author. With this in mind costumes, choreography and scenography must not resemble in any way those of the original production. If the intention is indeed to replicate the original work, that must be declared to PRS. They will decide whether they can liaise with the author to gain permission or suggest ways for the school to approach the author directly.

Mechanical reproduction

Following a successful dance recital a school may choose to record the event in the form of a DVD for parents and other interested parties. Merchandising a dance recital can be a source of additional income for a dance school but care must be taken to ensure that there are no legal infringements. Where a small number of copies are made, (in the region of around 200) a Limited Manufacture Licence would be necessary. Larger amounts of copies would require a DVD1 Licence. Both licences cater for free and sold DVDs or CDs. Both licences are available from PRS. Where a DVD is published on YouTube for entertainment purposes, it would be covered by the license owned by YouTube. But it is important to note that circumstances change if the DVD is used for promotional or financial gain. In such cases, all music that is recorded on the DVD and subsequently used for monetary gain online would require the permission of the relevant artists. Depending on the policies held by the artist or publisher a number of things may happen. Failure to get permission could result in the footage being subject to a copyright infringement notice resulting in a YouTube ID Claim. This may include the DVD being deleted completely. Alternatively music companies may choose to benefit from the infringement by claiming all advertising revenue and getting it redirected to the music author.

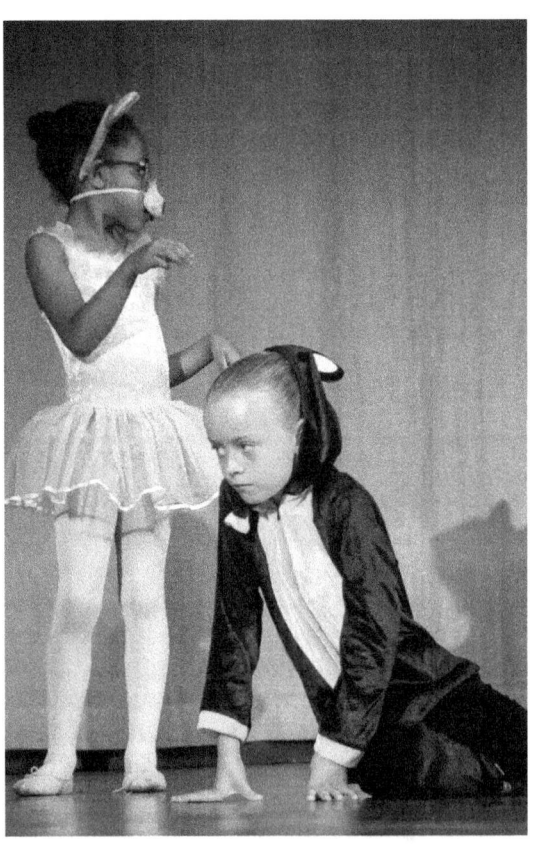

The Curtain Call

The curtain call is a traditional and important component of the recital. It informs the audience that the show has come to an end and there is no more to be seen. The curtain call is a time when performers acknowledge the audience and thank them for watching. The lights go up, and if the house lights go up too, the performers are able to see the audience clearly in the auditorium. The audience can see all performers on stage and clap as a gesture of approval and thanks.

The curtain call can be performed in a variety of ways. Often, performers return to the stage when the show has been completed and take a bow in unison. A variation may involve ushering all pupils on stage at the same time, to perform a very basic dance routine for all of the performers followed by a simple exit off stage. The length of the dance routine should last about 32 counts or thereabouts. At the end of the piece all pupils join hands, raise them to the air and take two or three simple bows initiated by one of the downstage dancers. After this, row by row the dancers exit off the stage or remain on stage for award presentations to follow. This method is particularly effective where there are lots of very young children with little or no performance experience.

An alternative option is to have each dancer perform their own inimitable bow. Each dancer moves forward to centre stage and improvises for ten to twenty seconds, takes a simple bow or curtsey and returns back in line with the rest of the group. Each dance should be unique, entertaining and the dancer should be discouraged from prolonging his/her time centre stage. The dance should represent the dancer as opposed to the show giving the audience a little insight into the dancer's personality and talents. When each of the dancers have performed centre stage, they should all join in unison to perform a closing bow where the curtain call concludes. Despite being exceptionally entertaining this type of curtain call can be time consuming and may not be financially worth the extra time in the theatre. In general this latter option works well with small schools or big schools with big budgets. But if implemented well, the outcome for the audience is that every second on stage is maximised with dance entertainment. It is also quite refreshing to see improvisation after an evening of set choreography. If budget and time permits this option is most favoured.

It is customary for the most prominent dancers to enter onstage last of all during a curtain call. Where children are involved each group or individual dancer should be carefully lined up back stage with their chaperones. At the required moment, the group should filter onto the stage to take their bow as choreographed.

Sometimes the curtain call is overlooked and its inclusion is quick and to the point. Other times it is under-rehearsed and with all the work that has gone into the overall show, it is extremely disappointing to see pupils bumping into each other, a confused entrance order and a poor culmination of an otherwise well prepared performance. Taking due care and attention, a well-rehearsed curtain call will run smoothly and will provide an entertaining conclusion to a dance recital.

Marketing

The dance recital offers a school the best opportunity to showcase its work to the public. But for many schools the recital provides an occasion to raise additional funds and augment the school profile. During recital time, there are many ways to maximise the school's exposure to the public. Merchandising the company brand via videography, photography and award ceremonies all contribute to increasing public attention.

Merchandise

Branded t-shirts and sweatshirts, are a good way for pupils to commemorate the recital and are ideal as gifts. They help to consolidate the company as a brand, and each time the product is worn the item provides additional advertising. The recital title, the company logo and other information such as the theatre all contribute to making the product a uniquely branded purchase. It is recommended that t-shirts and sweat shirts are printed and produced on demand encouraging customers to pre-order wherever possible. However it is still necessary to purchase a small amount for the theatre to display and for audience members to view. The physical presence of merchandise will encourage sales while audience members are waiting to enter the auditorium. However is important to restrict the number of display goods available for sale. Once the new term has started, the desire for these products will evaporate and lose its purchasing appeal. Eventually they will be donated to the local charity shop, or sold off cheaply. A dance recital left with a glut of dance memorabilia could detrimentally affect its profit margin. It is imperative to review the sales figures for previous recitals and use that data as a yardstick for future merchandise purchases.

The Recital DVD

Most parents will want a professionally recorded copy of the dance recital if the option is available to them. These videos will be preserved for years to come for all the family to enjoy. The older the video becomes, the more valuable it is to the family. It will become the vehicle for nostalgic glimpses of yesteryear, permitting its viewers to recapture all the excitement of the recital performance. Subsequently, the DVD is a significant product on offer for parents to buy as memorabilia.

Parents may attempt to video recitals from wherever they are seated in the auditorium. But they rarely have equipment purpose built for the occasion. Often their attempts at recording are compromised by where they are seated. Poor quality videos are marred even further by dark shadowy heads bobbing indiscriminately in front of the camera. Last of all, having to view the whole performance from the viewpoint of a small camera lens can spoil the enjoyment of a live performance. Subsequently, the offer of a professionally produced video is irresistible for most parents when their children are involved.

From the school's perspective a DVD forms part of the school's dance heritage and will be viewed for years to come. It plays an important role in the school's dance archive and catalogues the school's performance history. In addition the recital DVD serves as a publicity product for marketing the school to future clients. It needs to present the choreographic works well and not be sullied by poor technical production.

A contractual agreement is made with a reputable videographer to capture the show. When the performance has been recorded, the film edited and transferred to disc, the DVD is sold to interested parties direct from the school or the videography company. There are video companies who will record the recital at no cost to the school. These companies hope to generate revenue by selling copies of the video direct to the public. Some videography companies have a sliding scale with the highest fees being charged to smaller schools who have less selling potential. Under these circumstances these companies usually operate with a minimum order to ensure their overheads have been covered. The bigger the school is, the cheaper the video is likely to cost as there is a bigger pool of clients to sell to. Other companies charge a flat rate with an agreed number of DVDs for sale included in the overall package. Under these agreements, the school is responsible for the sales and are free to order more copies if it is required. Some video companies also offer live streaming of recitals at a set fee as part of a package.

Organising a contractual agreement with a videography company is vital, to ensure no unforeseen issues arise. But the most important matter is to ensure that the DVD recording represents the school and the show well, and the production quality is of a high standard. A good videographer needs a keen sense of how dance moves through space and the ways in which lighting can impair or enhance choreography. The company also needs to know how a dance school needs to be represented, making good use of the highlights of the recital. The editing process should be fully exploited to create a look of professionalism and make the school appear dynamic, contemporary and an attractive option for new clients. The videographer should be equipped to video the show from a variety of angles in order to maximise the editing possibilities in production.

The DVD is a tangible memento that is treasured by performers, the school, family and the friends who elect to attend the show and buy the DVD. A poorly presented DVD could tarnish the memory of a recital, detrimentally affect sales and damage a school's reputation. By contrast a well-produced DVD may create revenue, improve the school's profile and provide pupils with a treasured memory of a childhood event

Ticket Sales

The most important avenue a studio will have to promote the end of year recital will be via the pupils who attend the school regularly. Friends and family are responsible for the majority of sales at a recital, and a few other recruits through general advertising. As such the number of pupils who attend the studio classes will give you a fairly good guide as to how many you can expect to perform in the recital. This calculation can also be used to estimate roughly how many ticket sales will be made. This information is very important because it can be utilised to calculate the potential revenue for the recital as a whole. This data is significant because it gives you an approximate budget to work with. It helps when deciding which theatre to use, which costumes can be purchased and the funds available for advertising and promotion. Using this information may also help schools to estimate the potential margin for profit when all the overheads have been covered. If the figures do not measure up, or the school is still in its infancy it might be better to produce a recital once every two years, giving the school time to grow. Alternatively, the school may need to source other means to generate funds; local charity events or council grants may be considered. However, a recital is an effective marketing tool that should be utilised whenever possible. Pupils should be encouraged to invite their friends and extended family members to watch them perform. Mums and dads don't generally require much persuasion but they too could be encouraged to invite additional friends and colleagues to the show. Past students might also come to see their old peers perform and support the school. It is useful to send out details of the show to the school email database. Parents who are considering registering their children in the autumn may want attend the show to get an impression of the school and its work.

Recital Photographs

There is no doubt that parents will want to purchase a commemorative recital photograph. Before the children arrive at the theatre some parents will have already taken photographs. But once they are given professional proof copies to view, their amateurish photographic copies pale into insignificance. Employing a professional photographer can be a revenue source for a dance school depending on the contractual agreements made with the photographer. Many professional photographers specialise in recital photography and have a substantial portfolio to view before any affirmative decisions are made. They are skilled photography professionals who have a clear and informed understanding of the needs of a dance school when photographs are taken.

The recital photograph is organised into two different categories; live action photos and individual portraiture. For a photographer, portraiture is the most lucrative because the majority of parents are most likely to buy beautiful photographic portraits of their children in costume. The pictures are usually stunning but because of the controlled photographic studio set-up, they can be quite static and devoid of movement. Portrait photographs are often taken in a makeshift photographic studio setting. This may be set up in the studio at school, or in an empty space during rehearsals in the theatre. These photos are perfect as dance recital memorabilia and suitable for a portfolio headshot, but provide little information about the school and the dance recital.

The live shots taken during performance are extremely valuable to a dance school. Action photos taken live are able to capture the atmosphere and excitement of a performance. As such, they are ideal for future school brochures, for advertising, marketing and presenting the school in a vivacious and animated fashion. Live shots bring the school to life and connote energy, vitality and dynamism. Because live shots and portraiture have very different outcomes it is very much advised to ensure that the two types of photography are taken at a recital.

To profit from recital photography the school is given an agreed percentage of the total sale of all photographs. Some photographic companies offer the dance school all live shots free of charge with the percentage revenue being withdrawn completely. Photographic companies are happy to release live shots to the school at no cost because they are still free to sell these shots to parents and are fully aware that the majority of sales will be derived from portraiture. But because action photos have good marketing value, schools are happy to relinquish a commission in favour of a collection of action based photographs for marketing purposes. Many of the best photographs taken will be used for social media campaigns, website photography and the school brochure. To maximise the value of live performance photos, these should be used for social media sites and include all recital participants. Parents will be far more inclined to share the photos, discuss the show and talk with others about the school online when their children are in the shots. The social media buzz created by parents could spark the attention of potential new clients who were unaware of the school's presence. All photos should be marked clearly with the company logo and any other relevant information on each photo.

A good selection of recital photographs is invaluable. They can positively help to recruit more students for the autumn term and elevate the school profile. It is essential that a photographic company is selected judiciously. Check their history and any reviews. If the photographs taken are poor, the school risks loss of revenue, marketing material and an important component of the dance school's history. In addition, any poor photographs released for public viewing will reflect badly on the school's reputation.

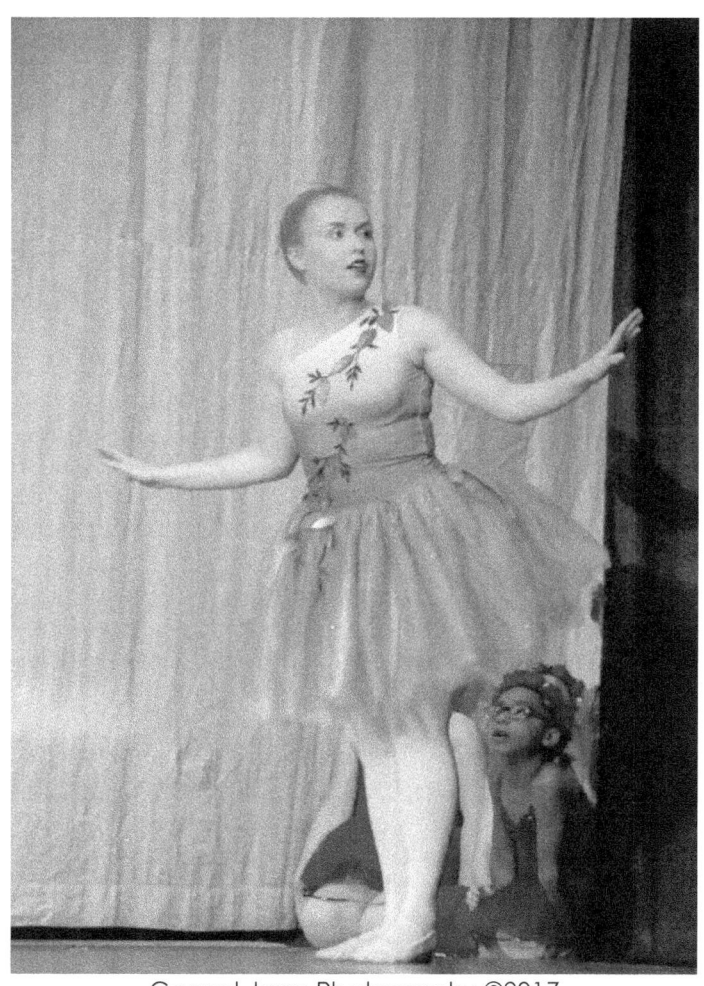

Carmel Jane Photography ©2017

Certificates

Certificates of participation or attendance are a great way to keep pupils motivated in school. It is a wonderful way to commemorate both the dance recital and give recognition to a pupil's dedication and commitment to dance training over twelve months. To receive recognition in the form of a certificate generates a sense of achievement, and can often spur participants to continue training with a school where motivation levels may be starting to wane. And whilst pupils should not be bestowed with multiple trophies and plaques to entice loyalty, a simple certificate provides enough recognition for pupils to feel a sense of achievement.

Many dance schools are affiliated to awarding bodies that offer qualifications that are nationally, if not internationally recognised. Pupils are encouraged to work diligently for these qualifications in order to attain good results that prepare the foundation for further qualifications from one year to another. For the serious dance student, recognised qualifications are most sought after. But receiving a certificate from a dance school offers a different type of validity. A school certificate gives a pupil a sense of belonging, a deeper kinship with other dance pupils and a heartfelt relationship with the teaching staff.

The optimal time to present pupils with certificates of attendance is directly after the curtain call when all pupils are on stage. In the presence of peers, teachers, family and friends a certificate award ceremony can generate a warm and nurturing environment for all present. The auditorium may be filled with endearing laughter as three and four year olds toddle forward keenly to get their certificates. Each child collects their certificate in their own unique way which is both charming and entertaining. The audience thoroughly enjoys this component of the recital. Parents love the opportunity to see their own child claim the stage as their own, if only for a minute or two. From a marketing point of view, the certificate ceremony has an emotive impact. The audience, the performers and all present become part of a special event that will never be replicated. As such the experience is unique creating fond memories that will be remembered for years to come by all who were there.

There are a range of certificate options available for dance schools. Certificates can be distinctive; designed especially for the school with its unique logo. Standardised certificate templates can be purchased on line leaving only the name and school to be filled in where required. The former is the superior option but the latter can suffice where time and resources may be a challenge.

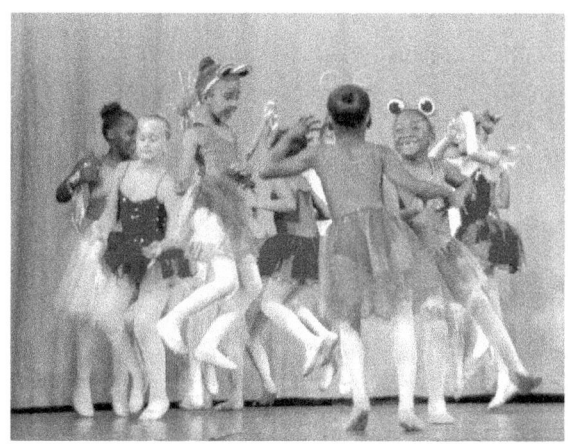

Carmel Jane Photography ©2017

Flowers

The presentation of flowers are a long held tradition at the dance recital. Flowers are presented to teachers and principals from their pupils. Parents give bouquets to their children and back stage staff may receive flowers from the school in appreciation of the time and support freely offered to the school. The flowers that are awarded to children from their parents are often an offstage affair. But on stage the presentation of flowers is a lovely conclusion to a well organised dance recital. It is a public recognition of unseen labour behind the scenes which would otherwise go unnoticed. Flowers are a public declaration of success, gratitude and teamwork.

Flowers are usually purchased before arriving at the theatre, but it is not uncommon to see a flower stall in the theatre foyer specially arranged for the dance recital. It forms part of the setting for the theatre foyer and may encourage members of the audience to purchase flowers even though they had not planned to do so. A flower stall needs to be arranged well in advance of the recital date, ensuring that there is a varied price range of bouquets catering to all budgets. It is generally understood that the price of a bouquet of flowers bought in a theatre will normally exceed the prices set in a normal florist's shop. Convenience, location and choice all contribute to the slightly elevated prices. But like all other products on sale in the foyer the quantity of flowers need to be carefully calculated to avoid making a loss due to oversupply and too many left unsold at the end of the recital. It might be useful to find out from parents in advance of the show whether they would prefer to purchase flowers in the theatre rather than stopping at a florists beforehand. Alternatively parents could be encouraged to pre pay for their bouquets and collect them when they arrive. This option is the most efficient for all concerned.

Curtains Down

There is always a sense of euphoria at the end of a recital. A good show will leave all its performers elated and riding high on success. The months of preparation seem disproportionate to the time a performance is played out in a theatre. But this is one of the markers of a triumphant performance; the time slips by without drawing attention to itself. Audience applause confirms that the show was well received and performers would happily do it all over again. The theatre is possessed of a buzzing energy that endures until the lights are turned off and everybody has left the theatre. The recital is done for another year.

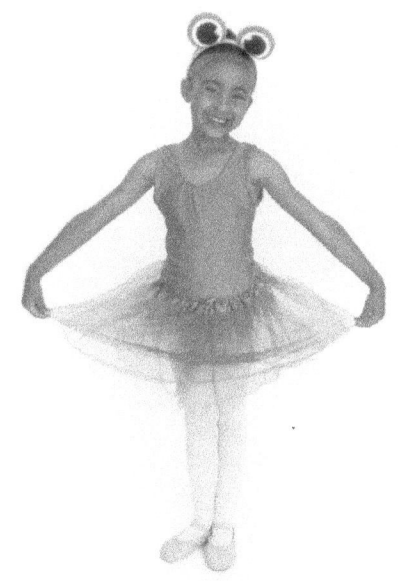

Carmel Jane Photography ©2017

Author

Judy John-Baptiste founded The Basement Dance studio in 1997, a dance studio based in the heart of London offering a wide range of dance classes to adults and children. She studied dance formally at Trinity Laban and gained a Master's degree in Performance Art Middlesex University. Her general education in dance was completed at Surrey University where she acquired a post graduate certificate of education specialising in dance training.

Ms John-Baptiste has worked as a choreographer and performer but has extensive experience as a dance teacher. She has written several dance courses which have received national accreditation with OCN a national awarding body in the UK. She teaches grade classes in ballet and jazz to children and adults in London alongside writing dance related texts.

Other books include: *Teaching Ballet Creatively, Allie's First Ballet Exam* and *Allie's Ballet Alphabet*

For updates, and all related information please go to the website: www.teachingballetcreatively.com

www.ingramcontent.com/pod-product-compliance
Lightning Source LLC
Chambersburg PA
CBHW070108210526
45170CB00013B/790